Deliverance and the Resurrection Power of Jesus to Set You Free

Susan Palacios

Copyright 2022 Susan Palacios. All rights reserved. This book is protected by the copyright laws of the United States of America. This book may not be copied or reprinted for commercial gain or profit. The use of short quotations or the copying of an occasional page for personal or group study is permitted and encouraged. Permission with be granted upon request.

Scripture quotations marked (AMP) are taken from the Amplified Bible (AMPC), Copyright 1954, 1958, 1962, 1964, 1965, 1987 by The Lockman Foundation. Used by permission. www.Lockman.org.

All Scripture quotations marked (KJV) are taken from the King James Version. Public Domain.

Scripture quotations marked (NLT) are taken from the Holy Bible, New Living Translation, copyright 1996, 2004, 2015 y Tyndale House Foundation. Used by permission of Tyndale House Publishers, a Division of Tyndale House Ministries, Carol Stream, Illinois 60188. All rights reserved.

Scripture quotations marked (TPT) are from The Passion Translation. Copyright 2017, 2018 by Passion & Fire Ministries, Inc. Used by permission. All rights reserved. www.thePassionTranslation.com.

ISBN: 979-8-9880883-0-1

Table of Contents

Chapter 1	What is Deliverance?	1
Chapter 2	Where on Earth are We and What is Here with Us?	11
Chapter 3	What are We Made Up of?	19
Chapter 4	God Has a Legal System?	25
Chapter 5	What are the Legal Doors the Enemy Uses to Enter Based on God's System?	31
Chapter 6	How Do these Demons Operate in Our lives? What are their Tactics?	57
Chapter 7	How Do We Defeat the Enemy and Walk in Victory?	75
Chapter 8	Practical Steps to Achieving Victory	91
Chapter 9	Examples of How Spirits Work in a Person's Life	101

Preface

Who am I and why am I writing a book on deliverance?

I am a Holy Spirit-filled servant of God who was baptized in the Holy Ghost in 2017. Very quickly the Lord began a work in me that moved me into the giftings of spiritual discernment, prophesy, and enemy detection. The Lord qualified me for this role in His church. My background is as a Baptist who not only didn't know about the baptism of the Holy Ghost and His mighty saving power but also never even knew there were demons until He showed me. He taught me about deliverance and showed me many ways in which the enemy works. After a short time, I began praying for people and they would feel free, thus beginning my ministry into deliverance, which has grown and resulted in many testimonies as to the true power of God. The Lord entreated me recently to write and publish this book to help educate His church on the enemy so that we all learn to overcome the devil's work in our lives and walk in the full freedom that Jesus purchased for us.

I dedicate this book to Yahweh, Yeshua, and the Holy Ghost, who have my heart.

Special thanks to Kevin Zadai, from whom I have learned so much about the Kingdom of Heaven, and also to Daniel Pontious and Charlie Shamp, who have both been instrumental in my spiritual growth and learning process. Thank you to Valerie Mezel, and Bill Smith from Bethel Church (now Encounter), who introduced me to the Holy Spirit and encouraged my spiritual growth.

Chapter 1
What is Deliverance

What is deliverance? Most people are confused by this term, having little to no understanding of the bondage that exists over mankind since the fall of Adam. Man had been given full authority and dominion over the Earth in the beginning by God upon his creation but following Adam and Eve's rebellion and fall in the Garden of Eden, they lost the covering of God, and they lost dominion over the Earth. Because God had given man dominion, when Adam and Eve were deceived by Satan, they unwittingly handed the authority over to Lucifer, otherwise known as Satan. The prince of rebellion became the ruler of the Earth and all upon it.

Genesis 1:26-28 *says: And God said, Let us make man in our image, after our likeness: and let them have dominion over the fish of the sea, and over the fowl of the air, and over the cattle, and over all the earth, and over every* *creeping thing that creepeth upon the Earth. So, God created man in his own image, in the image of God created he him; male and female created he them. And God blessed them, and God said unto them, Be fruitful, and multiply, and replenish the earth, and subdue it; and have dominion over the fish of the sea, and over the fowl of the air, and over every living thing that moveth upon the earth.*" **KJV**

Man was intended to have dominion over the Earth from the beginning of creation and was able to walk with God, having access to both the physical and spiritual realms at that time, and was able to communicate with both the spiritual beings and the physical creation beings.

John 4:24 KJV: *God is a Spirit, and they that worship him must worship him in spirit and truth. KJV*

We know before the Earth was created, God created angels and one of those angels was named Lucifer, whose original name was Helel. (Isaiah 14:12 Interlinear). Each angel has the name of God within their names, EL, such as MichaEL, GabriEL, and RaphaEL. The Hebrew word in Isaiah 14:12 is helel, which means 'shining one.' This cherub was the leader of worship to the Most High, leader over a third of heaven's angels, and basked in the glory of God's presence. Lucifer is referred to in Ezekiel and he was the second in command, right below the throne of God.

Ezekiel 28:12-19

You were the model of perfection, full of wisdom and exquisite in beauty. You were in Eden, the garden of God. Your clothing was adorned with every precious stone, red carnelian, pale-green peridot, white moonstone, blue-green beryl, onyx, green jasper, blue lapis lazuli, turquoise, and emerald – all beautifully crafted for you and set in the finest gold. They were given to you on the day you were created. I ordained and anointed you, as the mighty angelic guardian. You had access to the holy mountain of God and walked among the stones of fire. You were blameless in all you did from the day you were created until the day evil was found in you. Your rich commerce led you to violence, and you sinned. So, I banished you in disgrace from the mountain of God. I expelled you, O mighty guardian, from your place among the stones of fire. Your heart was filled with pride because of all your beauty. Your wisdom was corrupted by your love of splendor. So, I threw you to the ground and exposed you to the curious gaze of kings. You defiled your sanctuaries with your many sins and your dishonest trade. So, I brought fire out from within you, and it consumed you. I reduced you to ashes on the ground in the sight of all who were watching. All who knew you are appalled at your fate. You have come to a terrible end, and you will exist no more. NLT

In Isaiah 14 we see how Lucifer was not content with his position in heaven; he wanted to be LIKE the Most High and be worshipped as God. Because of his position and beauty, pride crept into him unchecked, and the first sin blossomed and grew into separation from God when Lucifer was expelled from heaven and thrown down to Earth, and then death, which is Lucifer's ultimate residing place in the lake of fire.

Isaiah 14:12-14: *How you are fallen from heaven, O shining star, son of the morning. You have been thrown down to the earth, you who destroyed the nations of the world. For you said to yourself, I will ascend to heaven and set my throne above God's stars. I will preside on the mountain of the gods far away in the north. I will climb to the highest heavens and be like the Most High. NLT*

Revelation 12:7-9: *Now war arose in heaven, Michael and his angels fighting against the dragon. And the dragon and his angels fought back, but he was defeated, and there was no longer any place for them in heaven. And the great dragon was thrown down, that ancient serpent, who is called the devil and Satan, the deceiver of the whole world—he was thrown down to the earth, and his angels were thrown down with him. ESV*

Satan was thrown down to Earth and continued his rebellion against the Most High by deceiving Adam and Eve with the same sin he was guilty of, which was wanting to be like the Most High. By eating the forbidden fruit, Adam and Eve unwittingly gave over their dominion over the Earth to the cunning serpent, who was Lucifer. He stole their dominion over the Earth, as he knew that their rebellion would result in separation from God, and a loss of their position of authority.

Genesis 3:1-7 KJV

"[1] Now the serpent was more subtle than any beast of the field which the Lord God had made. And he said unto the woman, Yea, hath God said, Ye shall not eat of every tree of the garden? [2] And the woman said unto the serpent,

We may eat of the fruit of the trees of the garden: [3] But of the fruit of the tree which is in the midst of the garden, God hath said, Ye shall not eat of it, neither shall ye touch it, lest ye die. [4] And the serpent said unto the woman, Ye shall not surely die: [5] For God doth know that in the day ye eat thereof, then your eyes shall be opened, and ye shall be as gods, knowing good and evil. [6] And when the woman saw that the tree was good for food, and that it was pleasant to the eyes, and a tree to be desired to make one wise, she took of the fruit thereof, and did eat, and gave also unto her husband with her; and he did eat. [7] And the eyes of them both were opened, and they knew that they were naked, and they sewed fig leaves together and made themselves aprons.

We know that Satan is the god of this world and that he controls this evil world system.

---

2 Corinthians 4:4: *Satan, who is the god of this world, has blinded the minds of those who don't believe. NLT*

I John 5:19: *We know that we are children of God and that the world around us is under the control of the evil one. NLT*

Romans 5:12: *When Adam sinned, the entire world was affected. Sin entered human experience, and death was the result. And so, death followed this sin, casting its shadow over all humanity because all have sinned. TPT*

Satan became the ruler of this world and set up the world system, which is corrupted and perverse, and contrary to God. We are all born as prisoners in this world encased in sin and under the power of Satan and his demons.

***Galatians 4:3** When we were juveniles, we were enslaved under the hostile spirits of the world. TPT*

The reality of our system on Earth is that Satan is the little g (god) of this world and controls this world system. Jesus came to the Earth to be the blood sacrifice that enables humanity to be removed from the evil world system under Satan's control and moved into the Kingdom of Heaven. While we will still exist in this physical realm, we will no longer be unwitting captives under the direction of Satan. The blood of Jesus has brought us back into the place of dominion that we had under Adam and Eve.

By the precious blood of Jesus which was spilled on Calvary to destroy the works of the devil, He defeated the enemy and all of his power and He transferred that power to His disciples.

Galatians 1:4: *He's the Anointed One who offered himself as the sacrifice for our sins! He has rescued us from this evil world system and set us free, just as our Father God desired.* TPT

Colossians 2:15: *Then Jesus made a public spectacle of all the powers and principalities of darkness, stripping away from them every weapon and all their spiritual authority and power to accuse us. And by the power of the cross, Jesus led them around as prisoners in a procession of triumph.* TPT

Luke 10:19: *Behold, I give you the authority to trample on serpents and scorpions, and over all the power of the enemy, and nothing shall by any means hurt you.* NKJV

The good news is that Jesus saved us not only from eternal damnation and judgment, but He also saved us from this evil world system that Satan has set up, and through His power and blood, we can be completely set free from it and sin and help others to do the same. How do we do this? This is accomplished in part through deliverance. The definition of deliverance is, in its religious usage, how someone who is possessed (or oppressed) by a demon (evil spirit) is delivered or set free from the bondage of the disobedient spirit. People who are oppressed can deal with physical ailments such as sickness and disease, as well as emotional ailments like depression, suicidal thoughts, anxiety, fear, panic disorders, addictions, and negative thought patterns. The demonic influence will lead them to engage in sinful behaviors such as rebellion, anger, revenge, hatred, conflict, jealousy, backstabbing, drunkenness, sexual immorality, idolatry, and selfishness to name a few. These are the fruits of the devil and those who are encased in the world system will display some or many of these behaviors in their life. Jesus came to destroy the works of the devil, and that is great news for us!

Chapter 2
Where on Earth are We and What is Here with Us?

Before we can examine the demon spirits and how they operate, we first need to understand the environment that we live in. Our physical senses can only perceive the physical world around us, but that is only one of the realms that surround us in God's creation. Three realms make up the world in which we live. There is the physical realm, the heavenly realm, and the demonic realm. There are layers to the heavenly realm, but for now, we will focus on the basics.

Philippians 2:10

The authority of the name of Jesus causes every knee to bow in reverence! Everything and everyone will one day submit to this name – in the <u>heavenly realm</u>, *in the* <u>earthly realm</u>, *and in the* <u>demonic realm</u>. *TPT*

Spiritual Realm (Encompasses Heavenly and Demonic realm)

The **spiritual realm** is made up of demons, angels, powers, and principalities in high places. This Kingdom realm is only perceived by our spiritual senses (there are five, just as our physical senses) which must be awakened and opened as we pursue the King through the covenant with Jesus and the baptism of the Holy Spirit. As we grow in our maturity of the spirit and our relationship with Jesus Christ, the Holy Spirit will open our spiritual senses, which will enable us to perceive and move in that realm. The Lord desires his church to move and operate in the authority and power that is bestowed upon us as children of God.

Angels

Angels are God's creation and have many purposes, such as glorifying and worshipping their Creator, but they also are referred to as Ministers of Fire.

Hebrews 1:7: *Regarding the angels, He says, "He sends His angels like the winds, His servants like flames of fire. NLT*

Hebrews 1:14: *Are they not all ministering spirits sent forth to minister for those who will inherit salvation? ESV*

The angels hearken to the voice of God and respond to His desire to bring His kingdom to Earth. Jesus defeated all powers of darkness on the cross and is currently seated at the right hand of God, ruling and reigning from heaven. The angelic assist the Lord in fulfilling His will and desire for those on Earth. These angels are all around us and respond to those who speak from the throne room as they listen to the voice of their Father. They want to help God's chosen ones and will assist His people by protecting them from the enemy and bringing God's will to pass in their lives. The angels are assigned to people, and they already know what is written in our books that God wrote about us before we were born. They are aware of when people are in rebellion and when they are obedient. They need our cooperation in being yielded to God to help us fulfill our plan and destiny. We need to cooperate with them by speaking God's word in our lives.

Demons

What are demons? They are the leftover hybrids from the age of the flood when God destroyed all humans and animals that weren't perfect in their genetics. They are unredeemable because they aren't human. The blood of Jesus doesn't redeem a genetically modified human. What was their main sin? SEXUAL! This is why there is so much sexual perversion in the world! They are manifesting in people! These beings were the result of the Nephilim and the interbreeding that resulted in giants and genetic mutations involving animals and people. The enemy had infiltrated the Earth and attempted to pollute the entire bloodline of Adam so that Jesus would be unable to come and redeem humanity. He had to be born to a pure bloodline, otherwise, He would be unqualified to be the pure, blemish-free sacrifice that would save humanity from the curse of eternal death. God, in His wisdom, determined that the Earth needed to be flooded to remove the offending mutations that infiltrated most of the family bloodlines at that time and the last remaining pure bloodline was that of Noah and his family. The Ark was not meant for all to come onto to be saved. It was a vehicle of salvation for Noah and his family so that the original bloodline of man could continue without the interference of the hybrid race. Through this act of the flood, God allowed the untainted bloodline to continue so that ultimately Jesus could be born of this pure bloodline and redeem the world. These disembodied spirits are unredeemable, and they hate all of humanity with a passion as we can be saved and are God's chosen race. The devil, using the demons, works tirelessly at bringing death and destruction to as many people as possible and to separate as many as possible from their true Father, God in heaven. Their mission is to exact revenge against God and to steal and destroy His beloved children. Jesus came so that His beloved children would be saved and live eternally with Him in glory following the end of this age.

John 10:10: The *thief comes only in order to steal and kill and destroy. I came that they may have and enjoy life and have it in abundance. AMP*

The physical realm encompasses everything we can see and experience with our physical body and physical senses. This is where the vast majority of 'the world' lives and carnal Christians as well. They have no awareness that any other realm exists, and they operate entirely on what they can see and experience with their 5 senses. In this realm, the flesh rules, and those who only exist in this realm are trapped in the devil's playground and are subject to the power that he has over the entire physical realm.

The **spiritual realm** is where the forces of angelic and demonic operate and where the principalities and thrones exist. This realm is actually far more significant than the physical realm, and this is the realm that God exists in, for He is a spirit.

John 4:24: For *God is Spirit and those who worship Him must worship in spirit and truth. NLT*

When Jesus walked on the Earth, he understood both realms and was able to access the spiritual realm, which is the realm of creation, and pull miracles down into the physical realm. Those Christians who are unaware of this realm are helpless against the forces that operate here because they don't even know they exist, despite the Bible verses that indicate the contrary. These evil spirits operate in secrecy and shadows. What better enemy than one you can't even see? As we move closer to Jesus through the baptism of the Holy Ghost, He will begin to open our spiritual senses and we will start to interact with the spiritual realm, where the power and authority of Jesus Christ resides. As He said in John 18:36, "My Kingdom is not of this world." We are seated with Him in heavenly places (Ephesians 2:6 NLT), "For he raised us from the dead along with Christ and seated us with him in the heavenly realms because we are united with Christ Jesus." This refers to his church residing in the spiritual realm with him and having access to the creative power and authority of Jesus that exists. The power of the spiritual realm supersedes the power of the physical realm, which is how Jesus walked on water, calmed the storms, turned water into wine, raised the dead, etc. Everything He did on Earth, he did as the Son of Man, not the Son of God, paving the way for His true followers to walk in the same power and authority by moving in the authority He gives us in the spiritual realm.

John 14:12 NLT: *"I tell you the truth, anyone who believes in me will do the same works I have done, and even greater works, because I am going to be with the Father.*

Jesus is the door to the spiritual realm as indicated in John 10:9 I *am the door, anyone who enters through Me will be saved and will live forever and will go in and out and find pasture (spiritual security). AMP*

However, you can also access the spiritual realm through Satanic means by witchcraft, sorcery, voodoo, meditation, Eastern religions, etc. The Holy Spirit is the master of the spiritual realm, and He is the only safe way for Christians to access that realm. Other religions have found a way to access this realm through drugs, meditation, chanting, satanism, and witchcraft, but those who choose this way are trespassers in this realm and ultimately will be judged as such. Accessing the spirit realm by means other than the Holy Spirit invites the demonic into your life. It is highly dangerous to move in that realm without the assisting power of the angelic beings or the Holy Ghost. You are easy prey for the demons to enter and take control of your mind and body if you enter without the blood of Jesus.

Chapter 3
What are We Made Up of?

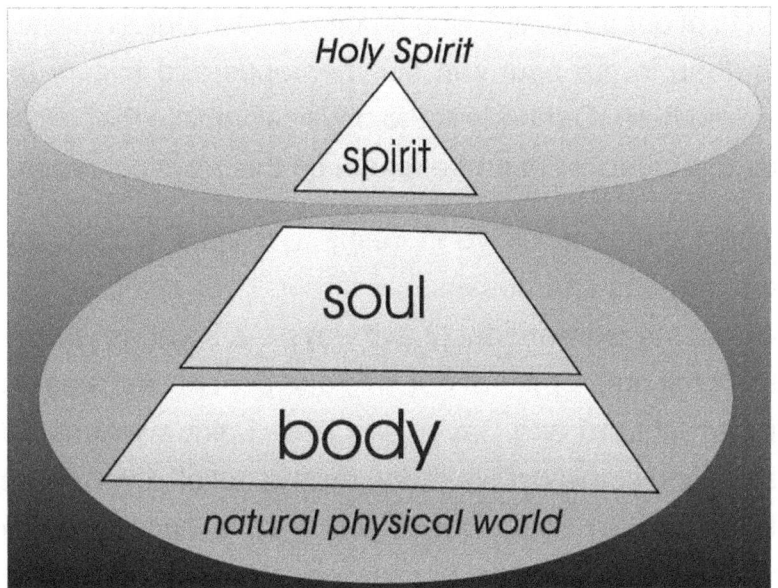

Spirit, soul, and body
___

I Thessalonians 5:23: *May your whole spirit, soul, and body be preserved blameless at the coming of our Lord Jesus. NKJV*

As humans, we are made up of a spirit, which is the divine part of us made in the image of God. We also have a soul, which attaches our spirit to our body, and consists of our mind, will, and emotions. Our logical thinking is done in our soul and our memories and history are stored here. Our body is the physical vehicle that allows us to maneuver in and experience this physical realm.

When one is not alive in Jesus, our spirit is dark, and the demons can possess us through our spirit, and we can act in extraordinarily evil ways. As soon as we turn to Christ and repent of our sins and accept Jesus as our personal Lord and Savior, the Holy Spirit awakens our spirit and comes to live there, driving out all demonic activity from our Spirit. Our spirit is what is made new, and we can no longer be possessed. However, evil spirits can also be present in one's soul (mind, will, and emotions) and physical body. Those spirits typically will remain until they are cast out through deliverance (breaking the legal entrance grounds) or through our close walk with God, who drives them out as we move closer to the throne of the Lord and come to an understanding of our identity and authority. Spirits attached to our souls will cause havoc in our minds and our emotions. Those spirits attached to our physical body can cause addictive behaviors to continue to manifest and we will wrestle with sin temptations.

Why do Christians need deliverance? I thought we were made new when someone comes to Christ.

---

2 Corinthians 5:17*: Therefore, if anyone is in Christ, the new creation has come: the old has gone, the new is here! NIV*

As mentioned above, the Holy Spirit comes to inhabit our spirit, which is the eternal part of us and the redeemed part. The body and soul are not, and the demons continue to remain in those parts until they are 'washed through the water of the Word' and forcibly ejected from us by the power of God.

Hebrews 4:12*: For the word of God is living and active, sharper than any two-edged sword, piercing to the division of the soul and spirit, of joints and marrow and discerning the thoughts and intentions of the heart. ESV*

It is the Word of God that separates our soul from our spirit so that our fleshly or carnal self can die. It is sharper than a double-edged sword and it reveals the intentions of our hearts. As the word of God separates us, our spirit becomes stronger, our soul comes to a place of capitulation, and we are no longer ruled by our flesh or by our carnal desires. The Holy Spirit within us desires for us to be holy and yield to His influence and movements so that we can be transformed into the image of Christ Himself. This process of an overthrow from the soul to the spirit is what distinguishes a mature Christian, one who is moved by the impulses of the Holy Spirit and has allowed himself/herself to be taken over by the Spirit of God who will continue the ministry of Jesus through their yielded lives. This work brings glory to the Father and the Son's influence over the person becomes cemented and the devil will lose the ability to influence that person to agree to his deceptions and lies. This is the fruit of the true freedom that the Holy Spirit bestows upon those who yield to the Spirit of Jesus and allow themselves to be transfigured and changed into the image of Christ. They don't hold onto their past or what was, but they become new creations who hold the magnificent treasure of the Spirit of God within them, leading to a transformation of their circumstances as they are transformed and begin affecting their environment.

Romans 8:6-8: *Now the mind of the flesh is death [both now and forever—because it pursues sin]; but the mind of the Spirit is life and peace [the spiritual well-being that comes from walking with God—both now and forever]; ⁷ the mind of the flesh [with its sinful pursuits] is actively hostile to God. It does not submit itself to God's law, since it cannot, ⁸ and those who are in the flesh [living a life that caters to sinful appetites and impulses] cannot please God. AMP*

Romans 8:14: *For all who are allowing themselves to be led by the Spirit of God are sons of God. AMP*

What happened to the Israelites?

Think about what happened to the Israelites when they left Egypt. Shortly after being 'rescued' they turned back to their idols of Egypt and sinned by worshipping the golden calf and through sexual immorality before Moses even made it down the mountain. They were brought out of Egypt, but they still had 'Egypt' in them. Their journey to the promised land should have taken a brief time if they would have received the truth and allowed themselves to be changed. Unfortunately, they clung to their unbelief and what they knew, and they were not allowed to enter the Promised Land. They had to go around the mountain over and over until they all died out except for the two who had faith (Joshua and Caleb) and those two were able to enter the Promised Land. This is a picture of true deliverance. Jesus can save us from "Egypt" or the enemy's possession as we receive His sacrifice on our behalf and enter into a covenant with Him. We must then die to ourselves and allow God to live in us. We are His expensive purchase – with His blood, so our lives are not our own! If we yield to Him and allow our fleshly selves to be crucified, then He will remove Egypt from us and will transform us into the image of Jesus. It is this process of yielding and crucifixion that removes the demonic open doors from our lives.

Chapter 4
God Has a Legal System?

God's system is perfectly just and holy. What happened to Satan and his angels when they rebelled? They came under punishment and were cast out… separated from God. What was man's punishment when Adam and Eve rebelled? They were under punishment and cast out… separated from God. But He had so much mercy to PAY the PENALTY, so we could be brought back into perfect standing with HIM. He paid the penalty for every sin, past, present, and future and He removed all accusations of the enemy against us through the work of Jesus on the cross. BUT it is the Holy Spirit who enforces the work of Jesus, and the enemy will not willingly give up any ground. Through the power of the Holy Spirit, we MUST force the enemy to leave and let go of all access points (legal or illegal!)

Although the law was given to Moses to show the people their sinful nature, the law was also a 'document' of God's legal system so the people would understand God's kingdom. Within the law were the promises that came with keeping the covenant that God was entering into with the people after He saved them from the Egyptians. Additionally, embedded in the law were the consequences of rejecting their covenant with God. He made His system quite clear in the layout of the blessings/curses that would be bestowed on people based on whether they remained faithful to God and their covenant with Him. He is a covenant God, and He cannot be who He is not. We can find a list of these in **Deuteronomy 28: 1-68.**

OBEDIENCE = PROMISES (BLESSINGS) - New Testament/Old Testament

- When we have faith in Him, we receive His righteousness
- He delivers His people from the yoke of slavery (Pharoah in Old Testament, devil following the shedding of the blood of Jesus)
- We will be his treasured possession and a kingdom of priests and a holy nation if we obey him
- We will have his presence and He will give us rest
- We will be holy because He is holy, and He has set us apart to walk with us

- He abounds in love and forgives sin and rebellion
- He will fight for us
- He will bless the work of our hands
- He will meet our every need
- If we seek Him, we will find Him (with all our soul and strength)
- He will not abandon us or forsake us
- Our personal commitment to the Lord leads to redemption and life
- We will prosper in all we do and wherever we go
- He keeps his covenant of love to those who love him and obey his commands (love God with all our heart, mind, and soul, and love our neighbor as ourselves)
- He puts His laws in our minds and writes them on our hearts
- He will answer us
- He will put a new spirit in us. He will remove our heart of stone and give us a heart of flesh and He will move us to follow His decrees and ways
- He will ransom us from the power of the grave
- We have been forgiven, sanctified, justified, and are being transformed into his likeness
- We have every spiritual blessing
- We are reconciled to the Father
- We carry the hope of glory in us.

DISOBEDIENCE = CONSEQUENCES (CURSES)

What oppressions came from disobedience in the Old Testament of Israel?

- Our towns and our fields will be cursed
- Our fruit baskets and breadboards will be cursed
- Our children and our crops will be cursed
- The offspring of our herds and flocks will be cursed
- Wherever we go and whatever we do will be cursed
- We will receive curses, confusion, and frustration in everything until we are destroyed for doing evil and abandoning God
- We will be afflicted with diseases, fever, and inflammation
- The skies will be unyielding and the earth hard as iron
- We will be defeated by our enemies
- We will be food for the scavengers
- We will receive sicknesses, tumors, madness, blindness, and panic. We will experience fear and be oppressed and robbed continually
- We will be sent away from His glorious presence
- Our eyesight will fail, and our souls will despair.

The demonic realm manifested these curses and troubles upon the people of God, and they still do as we engage in sin and rebellion.

Our sin gives the demons the legal right to oppress us.

In the Old Testament, the only person who was specifically mentioned as anointed to cause demonic spirits to flee was David with his harp.

I Samuel 16:23: *So it came about that whenever the [evil] spirit from God was on Saul, David took a harp and played it with his hand; so, Saul would be refreshed and be well, and the evil spirit would leave him. AMP*

Whenever there was rebellion, the demons brought the curses to life in their lives. We will reap what we sow. Not only did it curse the current generation of rebels, but the curses attached to the people's bloodlines were carried down to successive generations. The curses remained until someone, usually a King in the Old Testament time or a righteous Judge that God installed, repented on behalf of the people after realizing they were living in rebellion and that is why they were suffering. Once they turned from their sin and embraced the Lord their God, He turned His face towards them, and the curses were removed from their lives and the blessings began to be poured out per the covenant God had established with them.

We can see the curses manifest from the enemy in the book of Job. When Satan asked to sift Job to determine how strong his faith in God really was, once God gave His permission, Satan went to work bringing destruction into his life, using enemy raiders, tornadoes, and even fire. Job lost his belongings, his children, and even his health. The enemy was the one who wrought all of the destruction in Job's life. However, when Job didn't sin by cursing God, the Lord, who came to bring life and life abundantly, blessed him with far more than He had given him before.

Galatians 6:7-8

God will never be mocked! For what you plant will always be the very thing you harvest. The harvest you reap reveals the seed that was planted. If you plant the corrupt seeds of self-life into this natural realm, you can expect to experience a harvest of corruption. If you plant the good seeds of spirit-life, you will reap the beautiful fruits that grow from the everlasting life of the spirit. TPT

Chapter 5
What are the Legal Doors the Enemy Uses to Enter Based on God's System?

- Ancestral lines/sin
- Covenants made with the enemy through witchcraft, secret societies, paganism, religion, including Masonry, Illuminati, Catholicism, Mormonism, Buddhism, Hinduism, all false religions, and even Greek societies in colleges
- Rebellion including:

    Sexual immorality

    Lustful thoughts

    Pornography

    Chasing after things instead of God

    Manipulating others

    Hatred of those who get in your way

    Senseless arguments

Resentment when others are favored

Temper tantrums

Angry quarrels

Only thinking of yourself

Being in love with your own opinions

Being envious of the blessings of others

Murder

Uncontrolled addictions

Wild parties and other similar uncontrolled behavior

Galatians 5:19: Warns us: *"The behavior of the self-life is obvious: sexual immorality, lustful thoughts, pornography, chasing after things instead of God, manipulating others, hatred of those who get in your way, senseless arguments, resentment when others are favored, temper tantrums, angry quarrels, only thinking of yourself, being in love with your own opinions, being envious of the blessings of others, murder, uncontrolled addictions, wild parties, and all other similar behavior. Haven't I already warned you that those who use their "freedom" for these things will not inherit the kingdom realm of God?"* TPT

ANCESTRAL LINES/SIN

When I begin praying for someone during a deliverance session, the Holy Spirit will typically unveil the spirits and curses that are attached to their bloodline first. The types of spirits that are attached are dependent upon what types of sin and rebellion existed in that person's bloodline that has not been put under the blood of Jesus. For example, I have prayed for people whose families had engaged in slavery at some point in their past and I will usually find a powerful spirit of bondage that is attached to them. This spirit will act as a python spirit that constricts the person so that they find it extremely difficult to move forward or gain traction in many areas of their life. This spirit manifests the curse of bondage, and the person finds that they struggle to break into success, relationships, or even their destiny in the Lord. I have also prayed for people whose families were involved in the Masonic Lodge or the Illuminati and the covenants that their ancestors entered into were still active in their bloodline. All of the incantations and words spoken in secret meetings and rituals carry a power that is like witchcraft, which creates a negative power in the spiritual realm and remains attached to the person and their bloodline following them. Not only does it carry a negative power, but in these organizations, the person who belongs actively adopts curses over their organs, bodies, and even life as they take 'secret oaths' to never reveal information. Their lives become cursed, and many suffer sickness and death, not realizing they have cursed themselves.

I have also prayed for those whose family had been engaged in active witchcraft, whether as a warlock, satanist, black magic and voodoo practice, or just a 'white witch.' Witchcraft is quite powerful, and it remains around the person in their atmosphere, actively influencing the spiritual realm, and can manifest in the physical realm. When powerful witches and warlocks are in your bloodline, the active witchcraft surrounds you and draws negative situations into your life which bring great destruction. I find many people who have been severely abused as a child or suffered great torment and tragedies, have families who had practiced witchcraft in their past. In some cases, the Lord reveals contracts in which the warlocks had 'married' their children to the devil and those contracts remained in effect even to successive generations, especially targeting the firstborn. These cases of deliverance typically require a more aggressive fight to free the person. Additionally, when witchcraft exists, many times, physical manifestations in the person's life can occur, such as the visibility of demons, physical attacks on their body from demons, hearing voices, furniture moving, doors slamming, etc.

To get free from curses that affect your family, it is crucial to repent of your family's sins and break all covenants and contracts that were made with the enemy. He will enforce every single one of those contracts and he has a long memory. Most of the demons attached to people have been in their bloodlines for generations and they know everything about the family and the person, giving the demonic a significant advantage in bringing more chaos and destruction into a person's life.

CONTRACTS AND COVENANTS WITH THE ENEMY

As I mentioned above in the discussion of ancestral lines, many people have entered into contracts with the enemy. Some are obvious, such as embracing secret societies, actively pursuing pagan religions, satanism, witchcraft, shamanism, Native American witchcraft, and even simple deals with the devil to give allegiance to him if he gives worldly wealth and fame. These contracts will stand as enforceable throughout someone's life and even bloodline until they are verbally canceled and revoked by a person of that bloodline.

There are other less obvious ways to enter into a contract with the enemy, and these include celebrating demonic holidays such as Halloween, and reading or watching demonic movies, books, and music. You can be sure that Satan owns Hollywood and uses every possible cultural method to influence people through entertainment. We must always watch our gates, our eyes, and ears and protect our minds from demonic influences. Many people I have prayed for, who have opened doors through books, movies, or music, suffer from elevated levels of fear, anxiety, depression, and panic attacks. The enemy knows if we open ourselves up to evil then he can come in and torment us in our minds. This is what Paul has to say about how to live in peace:

Philippians 4:8-9: *"Finally, believers, whatever is true, whatever is honorable and worthy of respect, whatever is right and confirmed by God's word, whatever is pure and wholesome, whatever is lovely and brings peace, whatever is admirable and of good repute; if there is any excellence if there is anything worthy of praise, think continually on these things. The things which you have learned and received and heard and seen in me, practice these things and the God of peace and well-being will be with you." AMP*

The enemy knows he can influence us in our mind, so if we open ourselves up to scary things, negative or degrading lyrics in music, books, and movies about witchcraft or evil, then we open the door for mental torment. But if we focus on thoughts of what is beautiful and lovely and from God, then the enemy can't get a grip on our minds.

REBELLION

It has been established that rebellion allows for separation from God and torment from the accuser. When we are actively in sin, such as living in sexual immorality, or are drunkards, or watching pornography, committing adultery, lying, cheating, stealing, etc. it would be impossible to free ourselves from demonic bondage. Sin is an open door that allows the demons to torment us and if that door remains open then they will not leave. I won't even pray for someone who chooses to remain in active sin, because even if the demons are expelled, they will return and bring ones even more evil to live there and the person will be worse off than before. However, if we repent of our sins and remove the sin from our life, then the demons can be expelled. Typically, when someone begins with one sin and a demon is granted entrance into their life, they quickly become entangled in a host of sins as the demons work tirelessly to draw that person into deeper and deeper levels of rebellion. The demons especially enjoy when Christians become entangled in sin and open the door for torment. The demons capitalize on these opportunities and will manifest tragedies or sicknesses on the offenders with gusto. They despise Christians more than any and will torment them even more aggressively when given the opportunity. I have found, interestingly, that so many Christians that I pray for have engaged in sin and then have had traumas and tragedies occur to them and their family and they wonder why God hasn't saved them and why He doesn't answer their prayers. How is this even possible that they would expect God to free them when they have been in rebellion? Sadly, then, many times these people will blame God (pointing a finger at the wrong being!) and sink even further into their destructive situation. However, praise God, that once we repent of our sins, He is faithful and just to forgive us of our sins and cleanse us from all unrighteousness! When we repent and break the agreement with what we did, then we can cast off any demonic presence that came in from that activity.

I want to say a word about emotions and how the enemy will use them if we let him. Emotions aren't inherently bad, as God bestowed upon His creation the ability to feel emotions and free will in how to react. It is God's will that we all come to a place where we live in perfect peace no matter what happens or what the situation is around us. That happens as we allow God to heal our heart-wounding that has occurred in our lives and remove mindsets and behavioral patterns that resulted from that wounding. Based on our history, it is natural for us to feel certain ways depending on what is going on in our lives. For example, if someone hurts us, it is natural to feel rejected or wounded and to want to strike out in response or shrink in fear, especially if rejection has been previously present in our lives. If we are running late, it is natural to feel frustrated or angry with ourselves for being late or others for appearing to get in our way as we hurry to wherever we are heading to. If a friend talks behind our back about us, it is natural for us to feel betrayed and hurt. If we lose someone we love, it is natural for us to feel grief and sadness. If things don't go the way we expect, we can feel frustration or hopelessness come in and we can act out of those negative emotions. When we experience these emotions, which are quite natural, it is what we do with those emotions that ultimately determines if we allow the enemy to come in legally and begin to torment us. A pattern of negative emotions can lead to strongholds that are created within us and these can draw more negative situations into our life that will entangle us in those emotions and situations. When we experience a negative emotion, it lets us know that we have an unhealed part of our soul that is being triggered. At that moment, the best response would be to experience the emotion and then release it to God and give it to Him. We can't allow it to settle in our minds or gain any traction with us. We don't want to agree with it. We can feel it, acknowledge it, and give it over to the Lord and refuse to hold on to it. If we can train ourselves to not allow temporal emotions to control our behaviors, then we can't be imprisoned within those emotions and reactions.

Other methods the enemy uses to legally come to torment us include the following:

- Demons also enter through trauma, abuse, unforgiveness, and wounding of the heart. Taking offense and conflict also open doors as well.
- Word curses over us (from others or yourself) allow the enemy to oppress us.
- Watching evil movies, listening to certain types of music, and reading certain books, such as Harry Potter, are also entrances the demons can enter through. We must watch our gates! *(Matthew 6:22-24)*
- Taking communion unworthily. (*1 Corinthians 11:27-28*)
- Holding bitterness, resentment, anger, unforgiveness, or jealousy against another.

➢ Believing lies the enemy sets up in us, such as being rejected, unworthy, an orphan, unloved, etc.

TRAUMA

One of the enemy's favorite tactics is to cause wounding of the heart in children by people around them through traumas, such as physical abuse, sexual abuse, or rejection-type behaviors that result in the heart being wounded and lies entering into the child. Those lies become strongholds of emotions in their lives, such as feeling rejected, abandoned, worthless, less than others, etc.

Whenever we have a distorted view of our worth because of what people have done to us, the enemy is residing within and operates in our lives based on the lies we believe, such as being worthless, being different than others, not measuring up to others, etc. The enemy will work with other spirits to continue to bring circumstances into our lives that confirm these lies and lead us down the path of self-destruction. Many people will engage in behaviors that will mask these negative emotions, such as drug and alcohol addictions, or sexual promiscuity, thus continuing the demonic cycle in their lives and bringing destruction to them and their families.

WORD CURSES

Another tool the enemy uses is word curses. When we speak negatively about someone, we are actually creating witchcraft in the spirit realm that will begin to manifest what we spoke. Witchcraft is not just incantations and spells that are uttered, it also can be hateful words. The demons are always waiting for us to speak so they can begin to work on what we say. Just as the angels are waiting for us to speak the Word of the Lord so they can begin to work on what we speak out.

Proverbs 18:21: *Death and life are in the power of the tongue, And those who love it and indulge it will eat its fruit and bear the consequences of their words. AMP*

James 3:5-6: *In the same way, the tongue is a small thing that makes grand speeches. But a tiny spark can set a great forest on fire. And among all the parts of the body, the tongue is a flame of fire. It is a whole world of wickedness, corrupting your entire body. It can set your whole life on fire, for it is set on fire by hell itself. NLT*

People who have a spirit of negativity attached to them, tend to indulge in word curses often over their families and their lives, creating a cycle of never-ending situations that bring destruction into their lives and the lives of those they curse. Also, speaking negative words about yourself, such as I am not good enough, I am stupid, I can't do it, and words such as these, also create witchcraft and curses against yourself, and the cycle will continue. The demons hear you and will bring more of what you are asking for to you, and they will use anyone in your circle that can be influenced to bring what you are saying to yourself. It is so important to watch carefully what we speak. As God created man in His image, just as He can create when He speaks, so do we. This is a heavy responsibility and one we must guard zealously. What we speak, we will create, first in the spirit, and then it will manifest in the natural realm. Make sure we are not enabling the demons to bring negativity to us! Speak the will of God over yourself and others and your mountains, and watch God begin to move on your behalf. The angels are waiting to hear God's word spoken and will move and act upon it when it is uttered. Jesus said in Matthew 17:20:

For truly I say to you, if you have faith [that is living] like a grain of <u>mustard seed</u>, you can say to this mountain, Move from here to yonder place, and it will move; and nothing will be impossible to you. AMP

When we combine our verbal words with faith the size of a mustard seed, miracles happen in the spiritual realm that will ultimately manifest in the natural realm. When we begin to understand the authority we truly have in Christ Jesus, we can begin to change circumstances around us because we are speaking the word of the Father over others and into our own lives, and those words carry life.

However, when we speak the words of the enemy over others or ourselves, the demons go about bringing death. It is so important to remember that we need to focus on and speak the desired outcome over a situation in our lives, or in that of a family member or friend, not what we see with our eyes. The devil will bring negative situations to you to have you affirm them and those situations will be brought to life. However, you can reject what you see in the natural realm, speak what God's will is and watch things turn around! I have seen it over and over in my own life! The devil will try to bring a sickness or symptom of one and I will reject it immediately. I cancel his assignment against me, and the symptom vanishes! That clearly shows that the only power the enemy had was to try to get me to agree with what he was showing me, but I don't have to! I have a choice to align myself with God's will and reject what the enemy is trying to show me in the natural world. This can be the same with relationships. The enemy can use someone to try to stir you up or create trouble through a situation. You can get caught up in it and agree by speaking negatively about it, thus allowing it to spring to life, or you can reject what the enemy is doing through a person and speak blessing. Watch God turn things around in an instant! A perfect example of this happened to me just today. My son is at a boarding school, and he started just 2 weeks ago. I received a call from him today in tears that the teacher had expelled him from the class due to his 'attitude.' My son has never had an attitude as he has been homeschooled and has not learned those ways. I told him we need to forgive the teacher and release him to God. I hung up with him and immediately began to pray in tongues and asked the Lord to soften this man's heart. Within one hour, I received a call from the teacher, and even though he began the conversation aggressively in defense, blaming my son, by the end of our call, he agreed to go into my son's room and apologize for being too harsh and make peace with him. My son called me 10 minutes later and was overjoyed because the teacher had gone in to see him and apologized, and not only that, he gave him his phone number and said he could call him anytime he needed him. Also, he would be checking in with him every day to make sure he was ok. Come on! If that wasn't God moving on my behalf, I don't know what is! Of course, I could have allowed what was happening to take me over and I could have spoken negatively about the situation and the teacher, which would have allowed the demons to run amok and continue this path of aggression and hurt. Instead, I stopped it all in its tracks by aligning with God and giving grace. This is the power Jesus gives us! Another example of the power of our words and agreement just arose this past week. A dear friend of mine in Christ received a call from the doctor regarding her current bloodwork and was told she had to come into the office. This was unusual, but she went in to hear what they had to say. The doctor started speaking to her about HIV and that it wasn't as bad as it used to be and wasn't a death sentence anymore. She was told that her test showed her positive for it, and the doctor explained how one could get it. My friend was confused for a moment, then she said, "No, I don't have that. I reject that in the name of Jesus. This is a weapon from the enemy, and I refuse to accept it." While she was with the doctor and her blood results were on the computer, miraculously the test results went from positive to negative RIGHT IN FRONT OF THE DOCTOR. The doctor was out of her mind in shock and requested another test. My friend submitted to another test and the same thing happened. Although the initial result was positive, when she returned to the office the next day to discuss it, the results changed on the screen. Three tests later and the results are negative. This is the power of faith combined with speaking out a rejection of what the enemy is trying to do in our lives!

ALLOWING EVIL INTO OUR GATES

I always receive a lot of pushback from this teaching because people don't want to believe that enjoying what is common in our culture can actually be the very thing allowing the enemy to oppress them.

Matthew 6:22 TPT: *The eyes of your spirit allow revelation light to enter into your being. If your heart is unclouded, the light floods in!*

The eyes of our spirit are linked to our natural eyes as well. Whatever we allow into our natural eyes is going to impact our being, and if we are allowing things that are contrary to God, such as scary movies, which bring fear, witchcraft ideology through books such as Harry Potter, or dark or sexual spirits through certain types of music such as rap into our physical senses, then our eyes will become clouded and the enemy will enter through this door we have just opened by partnering with things that are anti-God. The demons know all of this and have taken over pop culture to deceptively influence each generation. The demons are integrated into the movies, the music, and the books, and by partaking in them, you are opening the door to them.

I Corinthians 10:21 AMP

You cannot drink [both] the Lord's cup and the cup of demons. You cannot share in both the Lord's table and the table of demons [thereby becoming partners with them].

We must discern what is pleasing to God and is of God, and what is of the enemy and steer as far away as possible from what is of the enemy. The enemy is always dishing up a delightful platter of something that excites the soul and the flesh because that is where man is entrapped and enslaved. The lusts of the flesh and desires of the eyes are man's weakness, and the enemy well knows this and uses it to his advantage to enslave people and oppress them.

Mark 9:47 AMP

If your eye causes you to stumble and sin, throw it out [that is, remove yourself from the source of temptation]! It would be better for you to enter the kingdom of God with one eye than to have two eyes and be thrown into hell.

Jesus made it clear that we need to remove those things from our lives that would lead us into sin and what we allow into our eyes and ears can absolutely lead us down the wrong path. The enemy is like a roaring lion, seeking whom he may devour.

---

1 Peter 5:8

Be sober [well balanced and self-disciplined], be alert and cautious at all times. That enemy of yours, the devil, prowls around like a roaring lion [fiercely hungry], seeking someone to devour. AMP

If we are aware of the devil's schemes, then we can avoid the pitfalls and traps that are placed in front of us, preventing the demons from accessing us and bringing destruction into our lives. Remember the covenant promises and curses from earlier in the book?

TAKING COMMUNION UNWORTHILY

Paul talks about this in 1 Corinthians 11:27-32:

²⁷ So then whoever eats the bread or drinks the cup of the Lord in a way that is unworthy [of Him] will be guilty of [profaning and sinning against] the body and blood of the Lord. ²⁸ But a person must [prayerfully] examine himself [and his relationship to Christ], and only when he has done so should he eat of the bread and drink of the cup. ²⁹ For anyone who eats and drinks [without solemn reverence and heartfelt gratitude for the sacrifice of Christ], eats and drinks a judgment on himself if he does not ⁽ʲ⁾recognize the body [of Christ]. ³⁰ That [careless and unworthy participation] is the reason why many among you are weak and sick, and a number sleep [in death]. ³¹ But if we evaluated and judged ourselves honestly [recognizing our shortcomings and correcting our behavior], we would not be judged. ³² But when we [fall short and] are judged by the Lord, we are disciplined [by undergoing His correction] so that we will not be condemned [to eternal punishment] along with the world. AMP

It seems to be common in churches today, to have regular communions, and most partake of it when offered without a second thought. There is danger in that! Paul teaches us that if we partake of the communion without examining our hearts to ensure we don't have bitterness, or unforgiveness resting there, or we aren't coming before the Lord with heartfelt gratitude for what the blood of Jesus has done for us, then we are inviting judgment, and this can even result in sickness or death. That is a sobering thought! The demonic realm is well aware of all of God's laws and ways (would it be that most Christians would be as enlightened!) and they stand ready to enter when someone opens the door for them, whether in ignorance or not.

HOLDING BITTERNESS, ANGER, RESENTMENT, OR UNFORGIVENESS AND TAKING OFFENSE

One of the most common ways that demons oppress people is when we hold onto these types of emotions against another person or situation. While it is natural to feel emotions based on what happens to us at any point in time, the enemy knows if he can capture us in those emotions, then he can enter and begin to set up home in those emotional reactions that people partner with and continue to hold on to.

TAKING OFFENSE

This has to be one of the most common tools the enemy uses to torment people. The enemy realizes that people inherently have a sense of fairness that they operate from, which is why, when we are treated badly or unfairly, we typically will have a strong reaction of offense or desire revenge to make a wrong right. However, Jesus himself tells us to 'turn the other cheek' when someone hurts us or 'give someone our coat when they take our shirt.' Why does he do this? So we won't fall prey to the enemy! If we get angry and take offense at that person over their hateful actions, we have entered into a contract with the enemy with those negative emotions, and not only will that relationship be cursed, but we will suffer from spirits of anger, mental torment, sadness, and other such as this which will keep us in bondage. When we are wronged, we must immediately release that person to the Lord and forgive them. That doesn't mean that we necessarily need to keep that person in our life, but we must make sure we don't hold any negative emotions towards them.

Matthew 6:14-15 Amplified Bible (AMP)

For if you forgive others their trespasses *[their reckless and willful sins], your heavenly Father will also* *forgive you. But if you do not forgive others [nurturing your hurt and anger with the result that it interferes with your relationship with God], then your Father will not forgive your trespasses.*

Jesus teaches us that holding unforgiveness, hurt, or offense against others prevents us from being forgiven, which allows the enemy to come in and continue to manifest more of those emotions into our lives. It also prevents God from moving on our behalf and bringing blessings into our lives. Unforgiveness and bitterness are so wounding to the soul, that cancer and diseases can grow unchecked within the body. I have found in my ministry that when doing deliverance and the person can truly forgive and release the offenders to the Lord, their soul becomes cleansed, and cancer often evaporates! Once the open door for the sickness is cleansed and removed, then the manifestation of the enemy can no longer remain in the body.

BELIEVING THE LIES OF THE ENEMY

Another favorite tactic of the demonic realm is to create situations in our lives that cause us to believe something that is not true about ourselves. If we are rejected, then we may begin to feel that we are not good enough, or don't measure up, and the enemy enters into that lie that we are holding in our hearts and sets up camp. He will work diligently to bring more of it to us through those around us. We also can find ourselves in adaptive behaviors to being rejected, such as withdrawing from people, lashing out, or becoming people pleasers. All of these behaviors attached to that lie will oppress us and cause misery. We must be extremely careful what we choose to believe in our hearts about ourselves and the people around us. The Bible is the Word of God and is our source of truth. We need to study what God says about us and align our minds with those truths! We must reject any thought that comes to us that doesn't align with what God says and command it to leave. Don't let negative thoughts find a home in you!

What does God say?

You are beloved: *"Follow God's example, therefore, as dearly loved children, and walk in the way of love, just as Christ loved us and gave himself up for us as a fragrant offering and sacrifice to God" (Ephesians 5:1-2)*.

You are a masterpiece: *"For we are God's workmanship, created in Christ Jesus to do good works, which God prepared in advance for us to do"* (Ephesians 2:10).

You are chosen: *"For he chose us in him before the creation of the world to be holy and blameless in his sight"* (Ephesians 1:4).

You are Holy: *"For he chose us in him before the creation of the world to be holy and blameless in his sight"* (Ephesians 1:4).

You are Forgiven: *"When you were dead in your sins... God made you alive with Christ. He forgave us all our sins, having canceled the charge... which stood against us and condemned us; he has taken it away, nailing it to the cross. And having disarmed the powers and authorities, he made a public spectacle of them, triumphing over them by the cross." (Colossians 2:13-15).*

You are New Creation: *"Therefore, if anyone is in Christ, the new creation has come: The old has gone, the new is here!" (2 Corinthians 5:17).*

You are Redeemed: *"In him, we have redemption through his blood, the* forgiveness *of sins, in accordance with the riches of God's grace"* (Ephesians 1:7).

You are Worth More than Gold: *"In him, we have redemption through his blood, the <u>forgiveness</u> of sins, in accordance with the riches of God's grace" (<u>Ephesians 1:7</u>).*

You are a Child of the King: *"See what great love the Father has lavished on us, that we should be called children of God! And that is what we are! The reason the world does not know us is that it did not know him" (<u>1 John 3:1</u>).*

Chapter 6
How Do these Demons Operate in Our lives? What are their Tactics?

➢ **The demons enforce curses that are attached to our bloodline by working with other spirits operating through other people to manifest the fruit of those curses into our lives. This work begins at conception.**

Whatever sins exist in our bloodline can manifest in our lives, starting when we are born. Many times, when I pray for someone, if there is abandonment or rejection in operation in this bloodline, their parents will often have gotten divorced, causing trauma to the child as the demons work to bring those curses into the physical realm. Adultery or sexual immorality in bloodlines will often cause the curses over relationships to manifest and marriages and families will be broken. If there is abuse or sexual perversion in a family line, many times children will be sexually or physically abused at an early age, thus continuing the curse that is over the family. If there has been murder in the bloodline, many times the person will experience violence or trauma early in their life as the demons of death and self-destruction will enforce the curse. The types of demons that are attached to your bloodline will often manifest the sins and curses that are present in a child's life or as the person grows up. The demons will work diligently to prevent the person from turning to Jesus, and if they can't prevent that, they will continue to impose curses on their lives to hinder their walk with the Lord.

➢ **The demons work through our emotions and our experiences in life. They focus on getting us to believe lies that we receive in our minds based on how we are treated or what is said/done to us as a child.**

This is probably the area where most people experience emotional torment. Many people have come to me, suicidal or ready to commit themselves to mental institutions because they can't escape the feelings of depression, self-condemnation, helplessness, hopelessness, or even identity struggles, including homosexuality and lesbianism. The demons always are after a person's identity. At all costs, they want to prevent humans from ever discovering that we are made in God's image and His beloved creation whom He wants to lavish all of His blessings and promises upon. These demons will use any method that is available to them based in the types of curses and sins in the bloodline, to twist and deceive a person about their true identity. They will bring torment and rejection to cause a person to believe they are worthless. If there is a sexual perversion in a bloodline, it can manifest as a false identity in the person, causing them to reject the natural order and embrace their false identity of being a gay person or now even questioning their gender. The goal of these evil spirits is to prevent us from finding the authentic identity God gave to us from our creation when He breathed us into our mother's womb. As long as they can deceive a person into believing lies about who they are, that person will be bound by a false identity. Freedom for a person can only be found in truth, where there are lies, the enemy will be found diligently working destruction in that person. Many times, when I am praying for someone, the Lord will show me they are operating under a false sense of self, sometimes from the trauma they endured, that resulted in them having to create a false front to protect themselves from the hurt they were experiencing. As we go through the deliverance, we remove the demonic attached to their false identity and they break the agreement with having to protect themselves and control situations and/or people, and then the Lord will remove that false sense of self and bring their authentic self back to them, resulting in an immediate feeling of wholeness that overwhelms them!

➢ **The demons speak to our mind implanting thoughts that we believe are our own but are suggestions put there by spirits standing behind us or within us.**

This is a common tactic used by the demonic realm when they know someone is susceptible to believing lies. These demons will stand behind us, telling us that we are worthless, that nobody loves us, nobody cares about us, that we should just give up and commit suicide, and that the world would be better off without us.

Remember, they hate us! These spirits want nothing more than to destroy us. They will want us to be offended when someone mistreats us, they will tell us to get revenge and pay someone back. They will encourage us to sin; why not, everyone else is doing it? What will it hurt if we just try a little bit? There are three voices that we can hear: our own thoughts, God's voice, and the demons. If we are not cleansed by the blood of Jesus and purified by the Holy Ghost, we most likely will be hearing our own thoughts and the demonic.

- **Sometimes we can hear voices in our heads or suffer from severe addictive behaviors.**

Many times, I pray for people that can actually hear voices telling them they are worthless or that they aren't really saved, or how could God love someone like them. Typically, when we hear voices, this happens when we have engaged in active witchcraft or strong ancestral witchcraft exists in our family line. The demonic power from these events is stronger in a person's life, allowing a significantly higher level of mental torment. Many times, these people are committed to mental institutions or placed on heavy dosages of antipsychotic drugs. The sad part is that the world can't offer a solution to their problem. It is all spiritual and can be broken by the power of the blood of Jesus.

> **They will make us feel unloved, unwanted, rejected, or a victim, and our behaviors from these feelings open doors.**

Many times, demons will manifest curses in our life that affect how people treat us and we will end up feeling depressed, and anxious, have panic attacks, or be hypervigilant about how we perceive others are acting towards us. To make matters worse, many people engage in behaviors to attempt to 'fix' their negative emotions, such as engaging in sexual immorality and control to feel 'valued', going into drug or alcohol addiction to numb the pain, becoming cold and heartless to avoid getting our hearts broken, or turning around and allowing the Jezebel spirit in to control other people and situations around us to try to change our reality. These behaviors allow the demons to enter and continue to reinforce the initial negative feelings that caused these behaviors. It is a self-defeating cycle. So many people are on anti-depressants and anti-anxiety medicines, but the reality is they are oppressed by demons and God already has the only real solution, and that is complete freedom through Jesus!

➢ **We may experience physical pain or sensations or have sicknesses or disease manifest in our bodies.**

Sometimes people can physically feel the demons on them in the form of severe headaches and migraines, which are demonic and typically due to witchcraft, or feeling like they are being 'squeezed' by something or like they can't breathe, which comes from the python spirit of bondage. If there are curses against our health due to covenants with the enemy, the demons can manifest sickness in our body through diseases or feelings of pain that seem to have no cause. If there is a curse of death over our family, then early death or accidents can be prevalent in a bloodline and manifest over and over.

➢ **If there is significant witchcraft or occult involved, there can be physical manifestations of levitations, furniture moving, and other bizarre occurrences in this realm.**

Whenever people actively engage the devil through Satanism, witchcraft, and the occult, the door for the demonic opens wide and portals are open that allow evil spirits to manifest in more aggressive ways in their lives. It is common in deliverance with these types of people to have severe manifestations of yelling, laughing like a witch, jerking, dropping to the floor, and slithering like a snake. When we willingly open a door directly engaging the enemy, we allow those powers to access us and everything around us. A tangible feeling of fear can exist around us, mental illness can result, and severe psychosis tends to be the result of those who have opened the portal. Deliverance involving these can be more involved and exhausting as the demons are never willing to leave the ground that was legally given to them in a person's life.

- **We may have anger or unforgiveness due to what others did to us – the demons capitalize on this and our bitterness and unforgiveness and desire for revenge allow the enemy to continue to control and oppress us.**

Romans 12:19: *Beloved, never avenge yourselves, but leave the way open for God's wrath; for it is written "Vengeance is Mine, I will repay," says the Lord* AMP and Matthew 18:21-35.

Did Jesus deal with demons on Earth? YES!

Jesus cast out a demon in the synagogue when the demon recognized Him.

Mark 1:23-28

Just then there was a man in their synagogue with an unclean spirit; and he cried out [terribly from the depths of his throat], 24*saying, What business do You have with us, Jesus of Nazareth? Have You come to destroy us? I know who You are--the Holy One of God!"* 25 *Jesus rebuked him, saying, "Be quiet (muzzled, silenced), and come out of him!"* 26 *The unclean spirit threw the man into convulsions and screeching with a loud voice, came out of him. AMP*

Demons recognize Jesus! There are no atheists in the spiritual realm!

Jesus delivered a blind and mute demoniac (restores his speech and sight when the demon leaves).

Matthew 12:22

Then a demon-possessed man who was blind and mute was brought to Jesus, and He healed him so that the mute man both spoke and saw. AMP

Before his deliverance, he was blind, deaf, and dumb. Afterwards, the man could see, hear, speak, and worship. Jesus can set your physical senses free as well as your spiritual senses.

Jesus delivered the maniac of Gadara (Legion)-

Luke 8:26-39

*Then they sailed to the country of the Gerasenes, which is east of Galilee. **27** Now when Jesus stepped out on land, He was met by a man from the city [of Gerasa] who was possessed by demons. For a long time, he had worn no clothes and was not living in a house but among the tombs. **28** Seeing Jesus, he cried out [with a terrible voice from the depths of his throat] and fell down before*

Him [in dread and terror], and shouted loudly, "What business do we have [in common] with each other, Jesus, Son of the Most High God? I beg You, do not torment me [before the appointed time of judgment]!" **29** *Now He was [already] commanding the unclean spirit to come out of the man. For it had seized him [violently] many times, and he was kept under guard and bound with chains and shackles, but he would break the bonds and be driven by the demon into the desert.* **30** *Then Jesus asked him, "What is your name?" And he answered, "Legion;" because many demons had entered him.* **31** *They continually begged Him not to command them to go into the abyss.*

32 *Now a large herd of pigs was feeding there on the mountain. The demons begged Jesus to allow them to enter the pigs, and He gave them permission.* **33** *Then the demons came out of the man and entered the pigs; and the herd rushed down the steep bank into the lake and was drowned. AMP*

Before this man's deliverance, he was naked, exceedingly fierce, unmanageable, constantly crying and cutting himself, seized and driven by demons. After his deliverance, he was sitting, not screaming; praising God, not cursing; dressed, not naked; in his right mind, not insane; a convert of Christ, not a captive of Satan.

This deliverance was actually dealing with a territorial entity. Jesus intended to destroy this entity to open the area up so the Gentiles could receive His truths and ultimately the ministry of the apostles. This convert was the first apostle as Jesus instructed him to go and tell everyone the wonderful things that happened to him.

Jesus delivered a mute demoniac:

Matthew 9:32-33: *As they went out, behold, they brought to him a dumb man possessed with a devil.* ***33 And when the devil was cast out, the dumb spake: and the multitudes marveled, saying, It was never so seen in Israel. KJV***

Crowds marveled! They hadn't seen anyone with this type of authority in their churches.

Jesus delivered the Canaanite woman's daughter which was shocking because her race was currently under God's curse. Genesis 9:24 *When Noah awoke from his wine [induced stupor], he knew what his younger son [Ham] had done to him.* ²⁵ *So he said,*

> *"Cursed be Canaan [the son of Ham];*
> [a]*A servant of servants*
> *He shall be to his brothers." AMP*

Matthew 15:22 -28: *And a [d]Canaanite woman from that district came out and began to cry out [urgently], saying, "Have mercy on me, O Lord, Son of David (Messiah); my daughter is cruelly possessed by a demon."* [23] *But He did not say a word in answer to her. And His disciples came and asked Him [repeatedly], "Send her away, because she keeps shouting out after us."* [24] *He answered, "I was commissioned by God and sent only to the lost sheep of the house of Israel."* [25] *But she came and began to kneel down before Him, saying, "Lord, help me!"* [26] *And He replied, "It is not good (appropriate, fair) to take the [e] children's bread and throw it to the [f]pet dogs."* [27] *She said, "Yes, Lord; but even the pet dogs eat the crumbs that fall from their [young] masters' table."* [28] *Then Jesus answered her, "Woman, your faith [your personal trust and confidence in My power] is great; it will be done for you as you wish." And her daughter was healed from that moment.* AMP

Jesus tested her faith first when He said, "It is not right to take the children's bread and feed it to the dogs."

Truth we can receive from this!

> Deliverance is for the children of God, but He makes it available to all who turn to Him and come to Him!

Jesus delivered a demon-possessed boy who manifested with epilepsy and seizures.

Matthew 17:14-18: *And when they approached the multitude, a man came up to Him, kneeling before Him and saying, Lord, do pity and have mercy on my son, for he has epilepsy, and he suffers terribly; for frequently he falls into the fire and many times into the water. And I brought him to your disciples, and they were not able to cure him. And Jesus answered, O you unbelieving and thoroughly perverse generation! How long am I to remain with you? How long am I to bear with you? Bring him here to me. And Jesus rebuked the demon, and it came out of him, and the boy was cured instantly. AMPC*

This event was immediately following their descent from the Mount of Transfiguration. Right after the glory of the Mount of Transfiguration, the enemy confronts Him. How often does the enemy attack you immediately following a glorious experience with the Lord?

Why did disciples struggle to cast out the demon?

1. Too little faith
2. Too little self-denial

3. Too little prayer
4. Too much bickering

Jesus was frustrated with his disciples because He wanted them to understand the authority He was giving them and walk in the same authority. He knew He wasn't going to be with them much longer and they still were not getting it!

Jesus healed a crippled woman on the Sabbath, much to the anger of the religious people.

Luke 13:10-17: *Now Jesus was teaching in one of the synagogues on the Sabbath.* [11] *And there was a woman who for eighteen years had had an illness caused by a spirit (demon). She was bent double and could not straighten up at all.* [12] *When Jesus saw her, He called her over and said to her, "Woman, you are released from your illness."* [13] *Then He laid His hands on her, and immediately she stood erect again and she began glorifying and praising God. AMP*

This woman was bent over because of a demonic spirit of bondage for 18 years. Following her deliverance, she was set free and could straighten up immediately!

Of course, there are many more examples of Jesus taking authority over the demonic realm while on Earth, and casting out demons was a primary method He used to heal and set people free.

In the Old Testament, a primary example of deliverance from bondage involves the deliverance of Israel from Egypt.

This temporal deliverance in the Old Testament serves as a symbolic representation of the spiritual deliverance from sin which is available only through Christ. He offers deliverance from mankind's greatest peril—**sin, evil, death, and judgment**. By God's power, believers are delivered from this present evil age,

Galatians 1:4: *Jesus Christ, who gave Himself [as a sacrifice to atone] for our sins [to save and sanctify us] so that He might rescue us from this present evil age, in accordance with the will and purpose and plan of our God and Father. AMP*

and from the power of Satan's reign,

Colossians 1:13: F*or He has rescued us and has drawn us to Himself from the dominion of darkness and has transferred us to the kingdom of His beloved Son. AMP*

All aspects of deliverance are available only through the person and work of Jesus Christ, who was Himself delivered up for us...

Romans 4:23-25: *Now not for his sake alone was it written that it was credited to him, ²⁴ but for our sake also—to whom righteousness will be credited, as those who believe in Him who raised Jesus our Lord from the dead— ²⁵ who was betrayed and crucified because of our sins, and was raised [from the dead] because of our justification [our acquittal—absolving us of all sin before God]. AMP*

... so that we would be delivered from eternal punishment for sin. Only Jesus rescues us from the "wrath to come."

1 Thessalonians 1:10" *and to [look forward and confidently] wait for [the coming of] His Son from heaven,* **whom He raised from the dead—Jesus, who [personally] rescues us from the coming wrath [and draws us to Himself, granting us all the privileges and rewards of a new life with Him]. AMP**

A large part of Jesus' ministry was the casting out of demons which set people free physically and emotionally from the bondage that they suffered from. Jesus came to undo the works of the devil, and by removing the demons from people, their bodies and minds were returned to God's original design for them. He had great compassion for the people and longed for them to experience the fullness of freedom from the chains that He knew bound them.

Chapter 7
How Do We Defeat the Enemy and Walk in Victory?

Jesus already has! BUT we must:

1. Be in a covenant relationship with Jesus
2. Be filled with the Holy Spirit who enforces what Jesus did
3. Understand our authority.

COVENANT BEHAVIOR

The first step involves Covenant. When we come into the Kingdom of God, we must understand the covenant that we are part of. Let's start with the Biblical definition of covenant. The term "covenant" is of Latin origin (con venire), meaning a coming together. It presupposes two or more parties who come together to make a contract, agreeing on promises, stipulations, privileges, and responsibilities. There are expectations on BOTH parties!

What is God's part? This includes all His promises in the Old Testament that we mentioned earlier in this book, plus what Jesus purchased for us through his sacrifice on the cross, which includes access to the Kingdom of Heaven, which is the spiritual realm. The Holy Ghost is master of this realm, and we must participate in this realm to manifest the power of God.

What is our part?

We must love and obey God with ALL of our hearts, mind, and soul, which is the number one commandment Jesus gave us. We also must allow our flesh to be crucified with Jesus and resurrected with Him by the power of the Holy Ghost. This 'crucifixion process' results in an inward transformation through a total reformation of how we think and act. As we yield to this purification of our souls and we yield completely to His spirit, Jesus can live through us, the living stones of His temple.

Examples of covenants today include purchasing a house, a car, or a marriage. In all of these examples, both parties are required to contribute to the covenant, such as in the purchase of a house; the current owner gives us the house and we pay the money for it, or if a loan is taken out, the bank gives the cash to the seller and we must repay the bank according to the schedule laid out. If anyone defaults on their part of the agreement, then there are consequences. Obviously, in the case of a marriage, both parties are agreeing to be faithful to the other and to love and honor them in all circumstances. If one person fails in this agreement, the covenant has been broken and destruction of the relationship often occurs.

The second step involves what I like to call John 14-ing.

John 14:12-17*: I tell you this timeless truth: the person who follows me in faith, believing in me, will do the same mighty miracles that I do – even greater miracles than these because I go to be with the Father. For I will do whatever you ask me to do when you ask me in my name. And that is how the Son will show what the Father is really like and bring glory to him. Ask me anything in my name and I will do it for you! Loving me empowers you to obey my commands. And I will ask the Father and he will give you another Savior, the Holy Spirit of Truth, who will be to you a friend just like me – and he will never leave you. The world won't receive him because they can't see him or know him. But you know him intimately because he remains with you and will live inside you. AMP*

John 14:2*: Those who truly love me are those who obey my commands. Whoever passionately loves me will be passionately loved by my Father. And I will passionately love him in return and will reveal myself to him.*

Vs. 23 – Jesus replied, Loving me empowers you to obey my word. And my Father will love you so deeply that we will come to you and make you our dwelling place.

In John 14, Jesus gives us a clear concept of what He is looking for. He wants to be one with us, to abide with us, to dwell in our spirit so that it is Him living His life through us, fulfilling our lives with Himself. To accomplish this, we must die to our old lives and allow God to manifest in us. What a glorious God we have who would give Himself to His children so freely!

We must also separate from the world system. To be free we cannot have one foot in the world and one with Jesus. We cannot pursue living in the spirit and continuing to satisfy our flesh by living in the world system.

John 15:18-19: tells us that Jesus has taken us out of this world…

If the world hates you [and it does], know that it has hated Me before it hated you. [19] *If you belonged to the world, the world would love [you as] its own and would treat you with affection. But you are not of the world [you no longer belong to it], but I have chosen you out of the world. And because of this, the world hates you. AMP (He set us free from bondage to the world system).*

Remember, Satan is the little g (od) of this world, and he has set up the system to influence people through culture, movies, books, and music. When we partake in these things that are not holy, the enemy gains legal rights in our lives.

Why don't many Christians feel free after salvation?

- Lack of understanding of the covenant
- Lack of understanding of the spiritual realm, the enemy's weapons, and God's eternal laws
- Never receive deliverance, whether through a minister or directly from the Lord as you come close to the fire of the throne
- Lack of understanding that we must reject the world system – we can't keep one foot in the world and one with Jesus – we must give ALL of our best (time, money, thoughts, etc.) to GOD!
- Lack of baptism of the Holy Ghost
- Lack of receiving and manifesting the true love of the Father which casts out all fear

> Lack of abiding in the Vine according to John 15
> Lack of understanding of our authority

Once we embrace the crucifixion of Jesus and receive His righteousness by faith in what He accomplished for us, we can receive the gift of the Holy Spirit who births a new life in us. As Jesus comes to live in us, our old identity is crucified with him if we yield to Him fully.

Galatians 3:20: *My old identity has been co-crucified with Messiah and no longer lives, for the nails of his cross crucified me with him. And now the essence of this new life is no longer mine, for the Anointed One lives his life through me – we live in union as one. My new life is empowered by the faith of the Son of God who loves me so much that He gave Himself for me and He dispenses His life into mine. TPT*

I believe this is where many of us get stuck in our walk with Jesus. We receive the water baptism and the Holy Spirit as an engagement ring affirming the covenant between us and God. However, most don't understand what is necessary following this initial adoption into God's family. After the water baptism, we must ask for the fire baptism. John referred to this in **Matthew 3:11 NLT.**

I baptize with water those who repent of their sins and turn to God. But someone is coming soon who is greater than I am – so much greater that I'm not worthy even to be his slave and carry his sandals. He will baptize you with the Holy Spirit and with fire.

"The Holy Spirit is poured out upon believers through the revelation and power of faith in Jesus" from **Galatians 3:5.**

The overflow of the Spirit, which involves a Pentecost moment of fire baptism in which a believer receives power, enables Jesus to manifest Himself in our lives, giving us a rebirth and the lavish supply of the Holy Spirit to enable the believers to live in the Spirit. The rebirth that accompanies the transition of a believer from the kingdom realm of darkness to the kingdom of light is absolutely necessary for a believer to be enabled to walk by the power of the Spirit and to wield the authority of a child of God. For the vast majority of the Western church, this process is missing. We stop at the water baptism, which is a repentance of sins, and where the Israelites walked through the walls of water. Most stop at this place of initial freedom but do not move into the place of removing 'Egypt' from us and moving into the promised land of the fullness of the promises of God. Paul tells us that Jesus dispenses His life into ours. He does this through the power of the Holy Ghost! Jesus wants to continue the ministry He began when He walked the Earth, and He accomplishes that as a believer yields to the power of the Holy Spirit and our rebirth that allows God's power to manifest in our lives and change the world around us. If this process is not done in a believer's life, we will go around and around the mountain as the Israelites did and will 'struggle' with Egypt within ourselves and not enter the fullness of freedom the Promised Land gives. Paul makes this clear in **Galatians 5:*16* TPT** *"As you yield freely and fully to the dynamic life and power of the Holy Spirit, you will abandon the cravings of your self-life. For your self-life craves the things that offend the Holy Spirit and hinder him from living free within you. And the Holy Spirit's intense cravings hinder your old self-life from dominating you! So then, the two incompatible and conflicting forces within you are your self-life of the flesh and the new creation life of the Spirit. But when you are brought into the full freedom of the Spirit of grace, you will no longer be living under the domination of the law but soaring above it. The cravings of the self-life are obvious: Sexual* *immorality, lustful thoughts, pornography, chasing after things instead of God, manipulating others, hatred of those who get in your way, senseless arguments, resentment when others are favored, temper tantrums, angry quarrels, only thinking of yourself, being in love with your own opinions, being envious of the blessings of others, murder, uncontrolled addictions, wild parties, and other similar behavior. Haven't I already warned you that those who use their "freedom" for these things will not inherit the Kingdom of God? But when the fruit produced by the Holy Spirit within you is divine, love in all its varied expressions, a joy that overflows, peace that subdues, patience that endures, kindness in action, a life full of virtue, faith that prevails, gentleness of heart, and strength of spirit, will be found. Never set the law above these qualities, for they are meant to be limitless. Keep in mind that we who belong to Jesus, the Anointed One, have already experienced crucifixion. For everything connected with our self-life was put to death on the cross and crucified with Messiah. We must live in the Holy Spirit and follow after him."*

This passage is so critical for one who desires to walk in full freedom to understand and one that most Christians are not taught. Once we receive the Holy Ghost who brings us a new life, we must allow our old self to be put to death. As Paul indicates, we will have two conflicting parts of ourselves working against each other. Our sense of self will want to continue with its life that promotes itself and its desires, but the Holy Spirit that comes to live in us wants to bring us a completely different way to live that causes us to yield to Jesus so He can live His life through us. So, a battle occurs, and many people stay in this battle and struggle with sin. The demons know this and try everything they can to prevent a believer from moving into the place where we have truly allowed our selfish identity to be crucified with Jesus and have given the Holy Spirit true and full access to our lives to do with as He pleases. The demons know that once a believer has yielded to the Holy Spirit, the Holy Spirit will crush the cravings of the self-life which are listed in the previous scripture, all of which allow the demons the right to oppress people. They fight tooth and nail against this transformation process within a Christian because once a believer is transformed and yielded to the Holy Ghost, the demons will have no power over that person. Many times, deliverance is necessary to remove the demons that are attached to a person that are allowing sin to hold a person hostage, but then the battle is within the person's will. Once a Christian has been through deliverance, if we don't understand that we must allow the Spirit of God to vanquish our old identity, then we can sow the wrong seed in our lives. This can result in a renewal of oppression from the enemy because if we continue to walk in our old identity and heart issues, the demons will return.

"Make no mistake about it, God will never be mocked! For what you plant will always be the very thing you harvest. The harvest you reap reveals the seed that was planted. If you plant the corrupt seeds of self-life into this natural realm, you can expect to experience a harvest of corruption. If you plant the good seeds of Spirit-life, you will reap the beautiful fruits that grow from the everlasting life of the Spirit." **Galatians 6:7-8 TPT.**

As we yield to the life-changing power of the Holy Ghost, the behaviors listed above will be vanquished from our lives, which all lead to death, and the fruit of the Spirit: love, joy, peace, patience, kindness, goodness, gentleness, faithfulness, and self-control will manifest in our life and our transformation will occur. The demons cannot attach to these behaviors because they are the supernatural attributes directly released into us from the Holy Spirit, who lives inside of us. Our body is the temple of God, purchased by the expensive blood of Jesus, and as we yield to His Spirit, He transforms us into His Israel and comes to make His permanent home in us. Once this happens, the demons have nothing to hold onto within us. This position is directly related to Abiding in the Vine as listed above on why people don't get free after salvation. This conversion process must happen!

AUTHORITY

And He called the twelve to Him and began to send them out, two by two; and He gave them authority over unclean spirits . . . And they cast out many demons; and they anointed with oil many sick people and healed them (Mark 6:7, 12, HBFV, see also Matthew 10:1, Mark 16:17).

Luke 10:17-20: *When the seventy missionaries returned to Jesus, they were ecstatic with joy, telling him, "Lord, even the demons obeyed us when we commanded them in your name!" Jesus replied, "While you were ministering, I watched Satan topple until he fell suddenly from heaven like lightning to the ground. Now you understand that I have imparted to you all my authority to trample over his kingdom. You will trample upon every demon before you and overcome every power Satan possesses. Absolutely nothing will be able to harm you as you walk in this authority. However, your real source of joy isn't that these spirits submit to your authority, but that your names are written in the journals of heaven* *and that you belong to God's kingdom. This is the true source of your authority. TPT*

TRUE CHILDREN OF GOD HAVE AUTHORITY

There is POWER in the blood of Jesus!

Ephesians 6:11-12

Put on God's complete set of armor provided for us, so that you will be protected as you fight against the evil strategies of the accuser. Your hand-to-hand combat is not with human beings, but with the highest principalities and authorities operating in rebellion under the heavenly realms. For they are a powerful class of demon gods and evil spirits that hold this dark world in bondage. TPT

- Belt – truth to strengthen you
- Armor of Holiness – protective armor covering your heart (Jesus says that the heart is the source of good or evil)
- Stand on your feet – be alert and ready to share blessings of peace
- Shield – your faith can extinguish arrows coming from the evil one

- ➢ Helmet – the power of salvation's full deliverance (mind is set free from lies of enemy)
- ➢ Sword – spoken Word of God
- ➢ Pray passionately in the spirit (tongues) – the most powerful weapon against the enemy!!

BUT ALWAYS COUNT THE COST!

Following Jesus and obtaining complete freedom will cost you everything! But you will gain everything in Christ!

Luke 14:26

When you follow me as my disciple, you must put aside your father, your mother, your wife, your sisters, your brothers – yes, you will even seem as though you hate your own life. This is the price you'll pay to be considered one of my followers. And anyone who comes to me must be willing to share my cross and experience it as his own, or he cannot be considered to be my disciple. So don't follow me without considering what it will cost you. TPT

Galatians 5:16-21

But I say walk habitually in the Holy Spirit (seek Him and be responsive to His guidance), and then you will certainly not carry out the desire of the sinful nature (which responds impulsively without regard for God and His precepts). For the sinful nature has its desire, which is opposed to the Spirit, and the (desire of the) Spirit opposes the sinful nature; for these (two, the sinful nature and the Spirit) are in direct opposition to each other (continually in conflict), so that you do not always do whatever good things you want to do. But if you are guided and led by the Spirit, you are not subject to the Law. Now the practices of the sinful nature are clearly evident: hey are sexual immorality, impurity, sensuality (total irresponsibility, lack of self-control), idolatry, sorcery, hostility, strife, jealousy, fits of anger, disputes, dissensions, factions, envy, drunkenness, riotous behavior, and other things like these. I warn you, just as I did previously, that those who practice such things will not inherit the kingdom of God. But the fruit of the Spirit (the result of His presence within us is love (unselfish concern for others), joy, inner peace, patience (how we act while waiting), kindness, goodness, faithfulness, gentleness, and self-control. Against such things, there is no law. And those who belong to Christ Jesus have crucified sinful nature together with its passions and appetites. AMP

I John 2:15

Do not love the world (of sin that opposes God and His precepts), nor the things that are in the world. If anyone loves the world, the love of the Father is not in him. For all that is in the world, the lust and sensual craving of the flesh and the lust and longing of the eyes and the boastful pride of life (pretentious confidence in one's resources or in the stability of earthly things) – these do not come from the Father but are from the world. The world is passing away, and with it its lusts (the shameful pursuits and ungodly longings); but the one who does the will of God and carries out His purposes lives forever. AMP

How do we get free? Through self-effort, struggle? NO!

I John 5:19

We know that we are God's children and that the whole world lives under the influence of the Evil One. TPT

Chapter 8
Practical Steps to Achieving Victory

But Jesus sets us free (and the Holy Ghost because where He is there is freedom).

---

2 Corinthians 3:17: *Now the 'Lord' I am referring to is the Holy Spirit, and where He is Lord, there is freedom. TPT*

STEP 1 – Leave Egypt and walk through the Red Sea.

Receive Jesus as your Savior and get baptized, pursue God and a one-on-one relationship with Him who is the Word.

Hebrews 11:6 – AMP: *But **without faith, it is impossible to [walk with God and] please Him**, for whoever comes [near] to God must [necessarily] believe that*

God exists and that He rewards those who [earnestly and diligently] seek Him.

Ask for the baptism of the Holy Spirit and consistently read the Word, which washes our minds clean.

STEP 2 –Allow the Holy Spirit to remove Egypt from you.

You want to avoid going around and around the mountain aimlessly suffering under the demonic powers. Many Christians stay in this place due to lack of knowledge and never cross the Jordan into the Promised Land.

Pursue deliverance from your past and nail your old identity to the cross! Jesus already paid the price for those sins and curses, so we must enforce them and remove the demonic attachments. Learn about the spiritual realm and access doors for the enemy which include ancestral sins/curses, idolatry, your mind (thoughts that stem from your heart condition), your lifestyle, your body, participating in worldly things (movies, music, books, witchcraft, your words, trauma, abuse, perversion, and others such as these). Anything you do that doesn't honor God is a potential open door for the enemy.

STEP 3 – Learn what is pleasing to God and pursue it.

Loving others unselfishly and loving Him.

How to implement Step 2?

It is always helpful to work with a deliverance minister as they have an anointing to discern spirits and cast out the demons, but you can also engage in self-deliverance through your pursuit of Jesus.

First, we need to understand what allows the demonic realm in. The first area to tackle is our ancestral doors. We all have a bloodline and ancestors who made choices in their lives that didn't line up with God's will for them. Those sins remain in the person's bloodline until someone forcefully deals with them and the resulting curses that came into the bloodline. Additionally, somewhere in your line were likely people who made covenants with the enemy in one way or another, such as engaging in witchcraft, pagan religions, etc. To deal with ancestral sins, **first, repent of the sins of your ancestors and ask the blood of Jesus to forgive those sins.** Next, stand in the gap for your family and **verbally break all agreements made with the enemy in your ancestral lines, known and unknown. Ask the blood of Jesus to break all ungodly covenants**

and the corresponding curses that came into your life because of it. Next, **command all familiar spirits (family) that came from your bloodline to leave in the name of Jesus. Close and seal the door with the blood of Jesus. Renounce all witchcraft in your family line.**

The second area to consider for freedom is taking a survey of your heart condition. Have you been hurt as a child and carry wrong beliefs about who you are? Are you carrying anger and bitterness about what someone did to you? Did you suffer trauma and emotional, physical, or sexual abuse?

If so, ask the Holy Spirit to help you forgive those who have hurt you and release them to God. He is our defender and judge. Let go of any bitterness as it will only poison your heart and body, and lead to diseases and depression. **Break agreement with any lies you believe about yourself. The enemy can only torment you if you believe his lies, so verbally break the agreement, and determine that you are going to believe what God says about you in His Word, not what your experiences taught you. Ask the Lord to come and heal your broken and wounded soul so that the works of the enemy within your heart will be removed and cleansed.**

Another area of deliverance involves our own sins and bad decisions in our lives. Any sin we willfully engage in will allow the enemy to torment us. **Repent of all of the sins you can remember and ask the blood of Jesus to cleanse you from those sins. Verbally break agreement with those actions you took and if sexual immorality was involved, break soul ties with each person you were with.** The joining of people sexually merges them into one, so each person you engage with sexually allows their spirits to enter you. **Break the ties and send back everything that came to you. Break agreement with all addictions and sources of sin in your life and command them to leave you. If you have engaged in any occult, witchcraft, yoga, Halloween, demonic movies, books, astrology, chakra work, crystals, Wicca, and things such as these, repent of those things and break the agreement with them. Command anything that entered you from those events to leave you in the name of Jesus. Ask the Lord to cancel and remove all curses that came to your life from those sins. Ask the Holy Spirit to fill every empty place within your soul and cleanse you with his purifying fire. Seal all of the work Jesus did in His blood.**

Practical ways to achieve Step 3 and remain free.

PATHWAY TO FREEDOM – Jude 1:20

- Pray every moment in the Spirit
- Build yourselves up on the foundation of the holiest faith
- Fasten hearts to the love of God and His mercy
- Be compassionate
- Be merciful with the fear of God
- Be extremely careful to keep yourselves free from the pollution of the flesh.

PATHWAY TO FREEDOM – Romans 12

- Let the inner movement of your heart always be to love one another
- Be enthusiastic to serve the Lord, keeping your passion for Him boiling hot! Radiate with the glow of the Holy Spirit
- Don't give up in a time of trouble
- Speak blessing, not cursing, over those who reject and persecute you
- Never let evil defeat you but defeat evil with good.

Romans 16:19-20 TPT

So, I want you to become scholars of all that is good and beautiful and stay pure and innocent when it comes to evil. And the God of peace will swiftly pound Satan to a pulp underneath your feet! And the wonderful favor of our Lord Jesus will surround you.

What happens to us spiritually when we don't stay focused on Jesus and His kingdom with all of our hearts?

Let's look at the churches in Revelation that Jesus sent warnings to:

- Ephesus
  This church started out on fire but abandoned their passion and love for Jesus that they had at the beginning and Jesus told them to do the works they did at first, otherwise He would visit and remove their lampstand.

- Smyrna
  The church here possessed treasure but were warned that Satan would test their faith and Jesus tells them to "Be faithful to the point of death and He will give them the crown of life."

- ➤ Pergamum
  Pergamum had issues with the corrupt teachings of Balaam, by eating food offered to idols and engaging in sexual immorality. Jesus threatened to make war against them if they didn't repent.

- ➤ Thyatira
  This church was accused of tolerating Jezebel in their ranks and her teachings of sexual immorality and eating food sacrificed to idols. Jesus gave her time to repent, but she didn't so He would cause her and her followers great anguish.

- ➤ Sardis
  This church was accused of believing they were alive, but were in fact, dead as He didn't find any of their deeds meeting the requirements of His Father. He urged them to change their ways, or He would come as a thief in the night to them.

- ➤ Philadelphia
  This church kept the message of perseverance so they would be kept from the hour of testing that is to come on Earth. He told them to "hold tight to what they have so no one could take their crown."

> Laodicea
> Laodicea was called out as being lukewarm and Jesus called them miserable, poor, blind, barren, and naked even though they thought they were rich and needed nothing. He warned He would vomit them out of His mouth.

Jesus was unhappy with most of these churches because they started hot but became lukewarm over time. When we allow that to happen, we become open to oppression from the enemy and our walk with Jesus falters. When we move out from underneath the shelter of the Most High by allowing other things to take over our minds and lives, we open ourselves up to demonic assault and the resulting destruction that comes with it.

KEY POINT IN HOW WE MUST KEEP OUR FREEDOM:

We must keep our love for Jesus boiling HOT through the power of the Holy Spirit and our DAILY communion with Him. Satan is always trying to distract us with fleshly things which only separate us from the Kingdom of Heaven, which is the supernatural realm. If our love is BOILING HOT, then the works of the flesh will not capture us, and we will not be polluted or pulled astray. We will fulfill the desires of the Spirit (which are to be holy and a temple of worship and service to the Living God) and not those of the flesh.

Ephesians 3:16-20 LOVE REVEALED IN US

And I pray that he would unveil within you the unlimited riches of his glory and favor until supernatural strength floods your innermost being with his divine might and explosive power. Then, but constantly using your faith, the life of Christ will be released deep inside of you, and the resting place of his love will become the very source and root of your life. Then you will be empowered to discover what every holy one experiences – the great magnitude of the astonishing love of Christ in all its dimensions. How deeply intimate and far-reaching is his love! How enduring and inclusive it is! Endless love beyond measurement that transcends our understanding – this extravagant love pours into you until you are filled to overflowing with the fullness of God. Never doubt God's mighty power to work in you and accomplish all this. He will achieve infinitely more than your greatest request, your most unbelievable dream, and exceed your wildest imagination! He will outdo them all, for his miraculous power constantly energizes you. TPT

Chapter 9
Examples of How Spirits Work in a Person's Life

This part of the book will be my own testimonies of what has occurred during deliverances where I was ministering. The Lord has revealed ways in which the enemy works through these meetings.

Spirit of Criticism

The Lord brought me into more understanding of the spirit of criticism. This is something that I have felt like I have had to deal with for quite some time. This critical spirit tends to come in when someone grows up feeling unloved or unvalidated by their parents or guardians (or even friends around them). As they feel separated from the world and like they don't belong, this spirit comes to continue that motion in their life. To 'survive' feeling unloved and rejected, the person will begin to become critical of 'self' and 'others'. They internally feel like they don't measure up, so they sometimes can become perfectionists or have ridiculously high standards for themselves and others. Outwardly they will begin to tear other people down around them so that they can feel 'higher' or more validated. They often begin a work mentality where they need to show their value through what they do or accomplish. Or sometimes they go the other way and just dive into drugs or sin, feeling as if it is hopeless. This critical spirit doesn't allow them to ever feel at peace and happy for others. If someone else receives a compliment or gift, it hurts them deeply. It feels like a rejection if others are rewarded in any way. They take things very personally even though the vast majority of the time people's actions have very little to do with them. They live in a super-sensitive place where they are looking for ulterior motives from others or signs that confirm their deepest dread – that they don't measure up. To break the power of this spirit, love must come and cast out all fear; the love of the Father that knows no bounds. The person who has an encounter with the Father, cannot hang on to the lies that the enemy has told him/her all their life. The lie is exposed, and the person can see it for what it was and can then choose to reject it and it can be cast off and all the spirits that go with it – rejection, loneliness, perfectionism, condemnation, false pride, low self-esteem, addictions, etc. Ultimately the entire human race is under the lie of rejection because we have been separated from the Father and we all feel that to some degree until we come to know and accept Jesus. Then the Lord sends His spirit of full acceptance.

Romans 8:15-16: *And you did not receive the "spirit of religious duty," leading you back into the fear of never being good enough. But you have received the Spirit of full acceptance, enfolding you into the family of God. And you will never feel orphaned, for as he rises up within us, our spirits join him in saying the words of tender affection, "Beloved Father!" For the Holy Spirit makes God's fatherhood real to us as he whispers into our innermost being, "You are God's beloved child." TPT*

Revelation of how spirits are interconnected and the soil of our hearts.

This summer, the Lord decided to give me a lesson in spirits as I began to weed a large flower bed that had been completely covered by grass and large weeds throughout the summer. So, at 8 AM I went out and began weeding. I had to use a shovel to dig out the large grass clumps and there were many. As I pulled up the weeds, in some cases they were single weeds that were easy to pull up by the roots. In other cases, as with the grass clumps, I had to use a shovel and fight to pull the roots up. With the grass, I had to claw at it as the roots turned sideways and into the ground; these were the hardest to pull up the entire root system and I had to continue to claw up the roots even after I pulled the grass up. This was backbreaking work, and I was sweating profusely after three hours. It was sweltering by now and I was so tired from having to fight with every weed. As I continued, I felt the Lord showing me that what I was doing was very similar to what I did in deliverance. It felt like the exhaustion that comes when I am casting out demons in some cases. It truly is a battle but in the spirit realm, not the natural realm. The Lord showed me that there are various levels of demons, with some having more authority than others. These roots I was wrangling with were similar to demons who had great authority and in the case of the grass, many demons were interconnected with each other, and I had to ensure I got all of them out, or they would grow right back. As I was pondering these things, I also noticed that some of the pretty flowers I had planted last year were not thriving this year and as I was pulling weeds from around them,

I noticed that many had weeds in the root system of the flowers, so they were now allowing the flowers to thrive as they were stealing all the nutrients and even choking them out. The Lord showed me that it is particularly important that we don't sow good seeds into bad soil. We need to allow the Lord to fully purify our souls and remove all of the rocks and roots of evil (weeds) from our souls before we try to plant good seeds, otherwise, it will always be a battle. The Holy Ghost will take our battered souls and remove all of the hurt, the wrong ideas we have, the rebellious thoughts and actions, and the injustices done to us if we are willing to allow Him to come and clean house within our hearts. If we repent and fully turn to Him who is the lover and keeper of our souls, He will be good and faithful to create in us clean soil upon which the fruit of the spirit can grow. If we try to move in the spirit without allowing this cleansing process, we will end up with a garden that looked like mine, with lots of bad fruit choking out the beautiful fruit God wants to grow in us. We must take the time to surrender fully to Him and allow this cleansing and purification in our lives, and in many cases having a deliverance minister help us to remove the weeds that are choking out our futures, and our destinies.

Testimony of a deliverance involving a spirit of sexual perversion

This is a spirit that often comes through bloodlines and will manifest in a person's life, often in childhood, through sexual abuse or rape. This spirit will work with other spirits in family members/friends to allow access to the child and begin the path to destruction that is their ultimate goal. When this spirit has manifested in someone's life, then other spirits will be allowed in as the child/young person feels angry, fearful, hateful, and rebellious because of what is being done to them. Evil spirits attached to those emotions will manifest in that person's life, changing their behavior, and many times self-protection rises. The child will engage in behaviors that will 'protect' them from this abuse, such as putting up emotional walls because they believe no one can be trusted, or even ultimately abusing others as they try to process the controlling and evil behavior happening to them by asserting it onto others. The controlled then becomes the controlling. These children will typically grow up to be sexually assertive and active at an early age as they believe mistakenly that their value has to do with their body and how they can use it to gain the approval of others. They can become quite manipulative and deceitful to satisfy their need for acceptance from other people. Of course, attached to all of this is a deep-seated shame at what has happened to them and in many cases guilt because they can even believe that it was their fault. Self-destructive behaviors will follow into adult life, such as addictions to alcohol, and drugs to 'escape' from their tormenting thoughts and active rebellion against authority as they take a stand against the control that happened to them in their early years when they weren't able to take control. It is also common that if a boy was raped by a man, the sexual spirit that accesses him will turn them against the natural order and he will become a homosexual. This error occurs because the trauma and the spirit of perversion twist their true identity and cause them to believe the lie that was forced on them early on through the rape. These attacks by the enemy are carefully planned and masterminded through those who can be used to do the devil's work, whether wittingly or unwittingly to turn the children of God against Him and cause them to wander down the path of destruction. The entire goal of these demons is to terrorize people from an early age so they will walk through a dark path and ultimately blame God for 'not saving them' when the abuse was happening and never turn to the only one who can save them and set them free. When these spirits are entrenched in a person, even if they do turn to God, they can (and in many cases do) suffer from addiction to pornography, adultery, lustful thoughts, sexual immorality, and even homosexuality/lesbianism. All of these behaviors, though, are tied to the spirit that is in them and the resulting lies they believe from the trauma/abuse they received as a child. They can be set free with deliverance as the spirits are ejected from their souls where they came in and the trauma is dealt with, and the resulting lies are exposed. Not all sexual spirits result in sexual abuse in a child, but still, many teenagers become addicted to pornography, masturbation, and sexual immorality, which opens the door to all sorts of destruction in their lives and relationships.

Paul tells us in **2 Timothy 2:21-22**: *If you keep yourself pure, you will be a special utensil for honorable use. Your life will be clean, and you will be ready for the Master to use you for every good work. Run from anything that stimulates youthful lust. Instead, pursue righteous living, faithfulness, love, and peace. NLT*

---

1 Corinthians 6:18: *Run from sexual sin! No other sin so clearly affects the body as this one does. For sexual immorality is a sin against your own body. Don't you realize that your body is the temple of the Holy Spirit, who lives in you and was given to you by God? You do not belong to yourself, for God bought you at a high price. So, you must honor God with your body. NLT*

Also, the Bible tells us **in 1 Corinthians 6:13-17**: *"But you can't say that our bodies were made for sexual immorality. They were made for the Lord, and the Lord cares about our bodies. And God will raise us from the dead by his power, just as he raised our Lord from the dead. Don't you realize that your bodies are actually parts of Christ? Should a man take his body which is part of Christ and join it to a prostitute? Never! And don't you realize that if a man joins himself to a prostitute, he becomes one body with her? For the Scripture say, "The two are united into one." But the person who is joined to the Lord is one spirit with him."* NLT

These verses tell us that sexual sin affects the body like no other since when we join ourselves to another (as a man and wife were destined to join together) we become one with them. That means that the spirits that are in operation in the bodies are allowed access to each other, thus opening the door for even more demons to enter our lives. We create a soul tie with the person that was involved in the sexual activity, and we become bound to them and the spirits in operation in them. In addition to these soul ties and bondages that occur, engaging in sexual sin prevents the Lord from using us for good works, as our vessels will have become polluted. He desires to keep us as special utensils that He can use as He will since our physical body is His temple, and He inhabits us and desires to come and make His home with those who genuinely love Him and adore Him.

To get free from these sexually influencing spirits, one must deal with the trauma that allowed them in and forgive those who hurt them, bind the spirits at that point and send them out, and verbally break the soul ties with all of those people that had sexual access to their body in their life. Then allow the Holy Spirit to come in and heal the wounds and purify the physical body.

These sexual spirits that affect a person early on in a child's life, actually become a portal for many other types of spirits to enter. As I discussed earlier, when sexual abuse happens, the child is traumatized and ends up believing all types of lies about themselves, such as being worthless, having low self-esteem, feeling violated, guilty, shame, anger, resentment, holding on to unforgiveness and bitterness, rejection, being victimized, feeling like they have to protect themselves through behaviors such as withdrawing from people, acting out through rebellion, false pride, perfectionism. All of these emotions and behaviors allow those types of spirits in, which work together with the sexual spirits to continue the path of self-destruction in a person's life. They have all of this planned and they work hard to manifest the curses in people's lives to keep as many away from God and their destiny as possible

When I am going through deliverance with someone, we go back to the time in their lives when these spirits gained access. We bring those feelings and traumas to the surface, which allows them to be released from the soul and allows the part of their soul that had to deal with this trauma to give vent to their emotions and release them so the Lord can take the burden from them. I have them break agreement with all of the lies/behaviors they engaged in to protect themselves, including sometimes even creating false personalities, and the Holy Spirit allows them to heal to forgive the offending people in their lives. I bind and expel the demons that gained access to them at that point in their lives and their power over this person is removed.

One example of a sexual spirit manifesting in someone's life is when Tina and I were going through deliverance (name changed for protection). She had been sexually abused during her early years by her father and other male figures in her life. Her parents were drug addicts who very rarely gave her love and affirmation, but instead, made her house a house of conflict, instability, fear, and abuse. She grew up afraid, but also incredibly angry, and ultimately, as a teenager, she turned to drugs/sex to fulfill the large gaping hole that was inside her from a lack of love and not being valued by her parents. As her rebellious behaviors grew, even more demons gained access to her mind as spirits of addiction, anger, and uncleanness came upon her, bringing her even further into the path of degradation and destruction. She felt completely worthless, but she came to understand that her body gave her power over men, so she became sexually immoral and manipulated many men to get what she wanted. Of course, it was always a cheap thrill and never validated her true worth. By the time she came to me, she had been divorced several times, had experienced all types of tragedies in her life including her finances and relationships, and was at this point suicidal and extremely self-destructive. Would you be surprised if I told you that this person was saved at this point and was even Holy Spirit-filled? This is proof that turning to Jesus and even receiving the Holy Spirit doesn't automatically set you free from all of the baggage of the past and the demonic powers that were working in your life. After a four-hour deliverance session, dealing with the ancestral curses, and traumas from her childhood, forgiving her abusers, and breaking her agreement with the lies she came to believe throughout her life, immediately she felt like a completely new person! All of her suicidal thoughts and depression were gone, and she felt light as a feather and on fire for Jesus!

Testimony of a deliverance involving a person who had a spirit of bondage

Another example of a powerful spirit in operation in someone's life that was causing destruction was Tim. Tim had an extremely emotionally abusive mother, from a baby onward, as she didn't want him and made it clear his entire life that he was a burden to her. She never showed him love or affirmed him, but instead physically abused him from an extremely early age. He grew up extraordinarily angry and resentful and ultimately ended up in extreme rebellion. He was so oppressed by her Jezebel spirit of control and manipulation, that he would hurt innocent animals as a way to try to release some of the hurt inside of himself. He grew up to be an angry young man who always wanted to fight with people and assumed the worst about everyone. His language became foul, and he became embittered and rebellious in all areas of his life. This bitterness was eating him from the inside out and it affected his relationships with his wife and children. He was emotionally unstable and unpredictable, and everyone had to walk on eggshells around him. The powerful spirit of python had attached itself to his life and held him in extreme bondage over his emotions and beliefs. His finances had been cursed and his emotional well-being was in a very deteriorated state. After praying with him over several sessions to remove the ancestral curses of anger/rage/murder and dealing with the early-year traumas and lies he had believed, he became what I would consider an entirely different person! His aura of anger/hardness had vanished, and he became relaxed, funny, and very enjoyable to be around. He felt like a vise grip had been released from his life, and the bitterness and unforgiveness had left him and he felt for the first time that he was free and could move forward in his walk with God in purity. He had some guilt for how he had treated his family, but the Lord released that from him and showed him that He gave him the power to walk in freedom from all that had occurred in his old self. When this type of deliverance happens, Jesus takes your old self with all of its sins, lies, deceptions, and curses, and He nails it to the cross (since He already paid the price for all of it!) and you become a new creation. This is the true experience of a new creation when you are no longer entrenched in the person you were before Jesus and before having the demons expelled from your life.

Testimony of deliverance for a woman who had a spirit of suicide.

Another spirit that I have seen removed completely from someone's life is the spirit of suicide. I prayed for a young lady, named Bessie, who came to me ready to commit suicide, even though she was young and had beautiful young children and a wonderful husband. She had been physically and emotionally abused as a child by her mother, who was in addiction herself and under severe bondage. She grew up feeling rejected at the deepest level and felt like she had to earn love and affirmation, by being good enough, and doing good enough. Inherently, she felt like she wasn't good enough, but being what people wanted her to be would allow her to feel valued, even though inside she was dying. As we prayed, the spirit of suicide and self-destruction came off and was attached to rejection and abuse, which also was lifted off as we went through the early years of trauma. People-pleasing spirits came off and perfectionism was removed, allowing her true identity to come forward. She had built a false façade over her true personality in an attempt to earn love and feel valued, so the Lord broke all of those walls down. As we continued with the deliverance, the spirit of Jezebel (controlling and manipulating as well as a sexual seductress) came up and was attached to her controlling mother. This spirit is one of the most powerful ones that I deal with and will typically cause a physical manifestation. Her body arched and she screamed as this spirit came out. Once these spirits were out and the lies were reversed, this woman received complete freedom from the spirit of suicide, and she became on fire for Jesus, and she continues today to experience the fruit of her relationship with Jesus! Praise the Lord for His mighty power to save!

Dealing with the spirit of Jezebel

This spirit is one of the most powerful spirits that I deal with and this one typically manifests physically in the person. It is also the hardest to remove because the person has come into agreement with this spirit usually in an attempt to protect themselves from traumatic events and people. In many cases, they don't want to really let go of this spirit. Jezebel is a spirit of control and manipulation, and sometimes of sexual enticement. This spirit will usually enter from a domineering or controlling mother or parent who wants to control everything about his/her child's life. Of course, the root of this type of behavior is fear, fear of failure, fear that things won't work out the way they should, etc. Fear will create a behavior that involves manipulating people or events to force certain desired outcomes on them. Sometimes this spirit will enter someone because their early life was out of control, with parents who abused them or weren't there for them, and to find a feeling of security, they will begin to control everything in their life, or even some things, such as what they eat, or don't eat. They can become obsessive and compulsive and perfectionists. They can hold themselves and others to extremely high and unattainable standards and become distressed or condemning when those standards are not met. They can become narcissistic if their basic needs of love and nourishment weren't met as an early child and be selfish and demanding of everyone around them. They can lie and deceive others to get reactions that they want or attention from others. The times I have dealt with the spirit, physically when I was calling it out, the person would fall to the floor and scream. Jezebel never wants to leave. In one instance, we were processing how this woman's mother had sought to control her and everything about her life, even into adulthood. Nothing she did was good enough, her mother was always condemning her for her children, her ways of doing things, her career, choice of husband. She was afraid of her mother, but also deep down resented her on a powerful level and was bitter. As we brought up those parts of her soul where the emotions resided and she confronted her mother (in the spirit, not the natural), she began to let go of the anger and rage, and resentment she carried. She began to see she allowed Jezebel in to protect herself from her mother and she also carried behavior that sought to control herself or others. She repented for allowing Jezebel in and to control her and broke the agreement with that spirit. I bound it and cast it out and it was an immediate breakthrough in her emotions that had her feeling completely free for the first time in her life. She broke the agreement with needing to please people or earn their approval and even broke the agreement with all of her expectations regarding others. She understood that she couldn't control anyone, and she was going to allow them to be as they were and this alone released chains that bound her to people negatively. Her life changed completely after this deliverance and her relationship with her mother actually reversed and her mother, while not knowing what happened in the spirit, saw her in a different light and began to stop criticizing and controlling her.

Deliverance involving an ex-Satanist who actively worked for the enemy

These types of deliverances are significantly more difficult due to the many contracts the person makes with the enemy while in Satan's employment. While I was praying for Johnny, immediately he went into physical manifestations and dropped to the ground, writhing like a snake. The level of agreements he had made with the enemy had allowed quite the host of demonic powers access to him and they were angry about the deliverance. In this case, his bloodline carried previous satanic agreements and witchcraft, which set him up at an early age to be set for destruction by the enemy. Abused early on and brought into witchcraft, the demons had a tight hold on him, and his childhood was wrought with all sorts of bondages and torments that nearly killed him, including ending up in a gang and serving the devil. He opened many portals for the enemy to enter through and actively cursed people for profit. However, the Lord had His eye on him, and He saved him from falling into hell. After this experience with the Lord, he became saved but his previous work with the enemy allowed him to continually be tormented in every way. Through the deliverance, spirits of bondage and python, witchcraft, and satanism were broken agreement with and expelled, but it was a battle. They never like giving up on one of their own. He continued to physically manifest as these powerful demons were expelled by jerking and shouting and even causing a manifestation of slithering on the ground like a snake. It took a good length of time because of all of the trauma that needed to be brought up, but praise the Lord, in the end, he was a new person. He has had to fight to keep his deliverance and the enemy continued to come after him, but he understands his authority in Christ and has learned to stand his ground. Now, I am sure the Lord will use what the enemy did in his life to turn it around on the devil and he will fight the hounds of hell.

What you can expect from deliverance is a feeling when you leave, that you are different and free. Most often, the testimony I hear from those I pray for is that they feel so light and free, their minds feel clear, and they are thinking differently than they did before. Within a few hours, they experience a tangible and powerful transformation of their mind and soul that physically manifests in a feeling of being a different person.

Only the Holy Spirit has this kind of power over the enemy since Jesus stripped the enemy of all power and authority by what He accomplished on the cross. The Holy Spirit is the enforcer of the covenant and of the blessings that Jesus achieved for us at the cross, so when we allow the Holy Spirit to minister in this way, all of the powers of darkness can be removed from someone's life, and they are free from every legal right the enemy had in their lives to enact destruction. The open doors are shut and sealed with the blood of Jesus, and the enemy will no longer be allowed to bring harm to the person. Praise the Lord for His mighty saving power!

Matthew 12:28: *"But if I am casting out demons by the Spirit of God, then the Kingdom of God has arrived among you. For who is powerful enough to enter the house of a strong man and plunder his goods? Only someone even stronger – someone who could tie him up and then plunder his house." NLT*

Colossians 2:15: *"And having disarmed the powers and authorities, he made a public spectacle of them, triumphing over them by the cross." NIV*

Jesus did this by forgiving all of our sins through His sacrifice. Colossians 2:14: *"He canceled the record of the charges against us and took it away by nailing it to the cross." NLT.* This was how he disarmed the spiritual rulers and authorities. So, by our faith in what Jesus did for us and by our turning to Him as our Savior, God made us alive with Christ by forgiving us and cutting away our sinful nature. Because of these truths, we can be completely set free from all demonic oppression and torment! Thank you, Jesus, for setting us free!

Actual Testimonies

"Also, I do want to say that your prayer over me was a true blessing, absolutely one hundred percent. Let me tell you what happened to my family. After our prayer, my niece and nephews began to heal miraculously from that ATV wreck. My niece was never supposed to walk again, and my nephew was never supposed to use that hand again. Well, she's running all over the place and he's moving his hand! My brother got a brand-new job that pays very well! My sister came into an inheritance and it was so bizarre how it all unfolded but we're talking half a million dollars! My sister-in-law was healed from cancer and my brother is taking her to church now and he is getting back into his calling, which I love! There are so many good things happening! All my sons are serving God and praying with me now and I got to see all of my grandchildren at Christmas time! So, I give God all the praise and glory for that, but I also want to say thank you, thank you, thank you, thank you for being obedient to the Father!" Eva T.

In this sister's life, the enemy had a grip on their family through ancestral curses, so we went after those in the deliverance session. The power of God showed up in a powerful way and He changed everything! That is what He does! I see it over and over!

"You prayed for me and two years later I have been able to start my own plumbing company. The spirit helped reveal to me that people I have never met could have compassion for my life and His will for my life. I wanted to share my appreciation!"

Jarrod M.

"All my life I have walked around with a heaviness I couldn't really explain, it was just there. After being prayed over, I realized how much spiritual warfare was over my life and today I was able to see the light of Christ beaming through every part of my body and mind, and a weight lifted off of me in a way that I can't explain to a doctor how profound it was! I was born for this day to be set free from the enemy and show Christ through my life. I feel taller, I have a completely different perspective. I have joy!"

Camille

These are just a few of the testimonies, but I wanted to reveal how powerful God is when we surrender to Him and allow our bodies to be used as a vessel by Him to minister to the body of Christ. He changed their lives completely and they become victorious over the enemy and began to walk in their power and authority!

Works Cited

"Deliverance Definition." *Bible Study*, https://www.biblestudy.org/beginner/definition-of-christian-terms/deliverance.html

Myers, Jeannie. "10 Beautiful Truths God Says about You." *Biblestudytools.com*, 19 Aug. 2022, https://www.biblestudytools.com/bible-study/topical-studies/beautiful-true-things-god-says-about-you.html#:~:text=10%20Beautiful%2C%20True%20Things%20God%20Says%20about%20You,Am%20Worth%20More%20Than%20Gold%20...%20More%20items

Isaiah 14:12 Interlinear: How Hast Thou Fallen from the Heavens, O Shining One, Son of the Dawn! Thou Hast Been Cut down to Earth, O Weakener of Nations., https://biblehub.com/interlinear/isaiah/14-12.htm

www.ingramcontent.com/pod-product-compliance
Lightning Source LLC
LaVergne TN
LVHW011424080426
835512LV00005B/244